100 WORLD LEADERS

WHO SHAPED WORLD HISTORY

KATHY PAPARCHONTIS

sourcebooks
eXplore

Copyright © 2001, 2023 by Sourcebooks
Text by Kathleen Paparchontis
Cover design by Will Riley
Illustrations by Westchester Publishing Services
Cover and internal design © 2023 by Sourcebooks

Published by Sourcebooks eXplore, an imprint of Sourcebooks Kids
P.O. Box 4410, Naperville, Illinois 60567-4410
(630) 961-3900
sourcebookskids.com

Originally published in 2001 by Bluewood Books, a division of The Siyeh Group, Inc.

Cataloging-in-Publication Data is on file with the Library of Congress.

Source of Production: Versa Press, East Peoria, Illinois, USA
Date of Production: August 2023
Run Number: 5033349

Printed and bound in the United States of America.
VP 10 9 8 7 6 5 4 3 2 1

CONTENTS

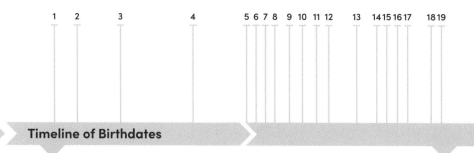

Timeline of Birthdates

2500 BCE   750

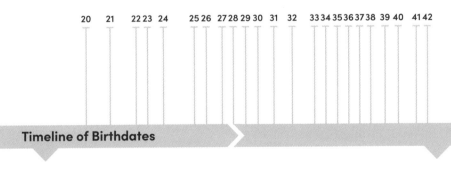

20 21 22 23 24   25 26 27 28 29 30 31 32   33 34 35 36 37 38 39 40 41 42

Timeline of Birthdates

750

1700

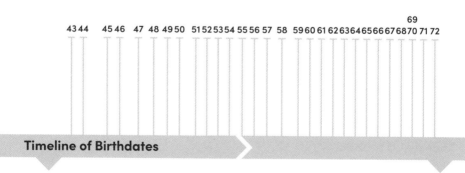

69

43 44   45 46   47   48 49 50   51 52 53 54 55 56 57   58   59 60 61 62 63 64 65 66 67 68 70 71 72

Timeline of Birthdates

1700

1885

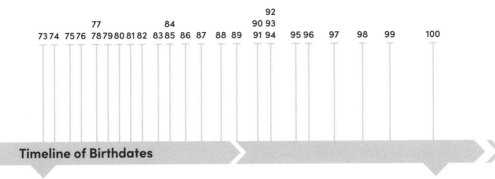

Timeline of Birthdates

1885   1955

INTRODUCTION

ANY AUTHOR attempting to narrow down an authoritative list of one hundred world leaders who have shaped world history faces quite a daunting task. After all, from the earliest days of recorded history, there have been thousands of people—men and women, young and old, good and evil—who have had a significant impact on the world. Where to begin looking? What qualities must a world leader possess? Must the title of world leader be only bestowed on someone whose influence stretched beyond the borders of their own nation, impacting the world at large? If so, what should we think about the leaders who made a significant contribution at a time when societies were much smaller than they are today?

In approaching this subject, we have taken a fairly broad view. Khufu, pharaoh of Ancient Egypt more than four thousand five hundred years ago, ruled a very small but very significant world. Lech Wałęsa, was once a shipyard electrician who rose as an activist to become founder and president of Solidarity, Poland's first independent trade union.

In between are ninety-eight other men and women who displayed the qualities—both good and bad—that enabled them to leave an imprint on history. Of course, the requirements to become a world leader have changed dramatically over the centuries. For nearly one thousand years, world leaders were men who achieved great power through conquest. They often began with their own lands, and then spread their influence by dominating other nations and their peoples. Men such as Alexander the Great, Julius Caesar, Attila, William the Conqueror, and Genghis Khan would fit into this category. All these leaders combined military and political skills to dominate their eras—though some for only a brief time—and leave an indelible mark on the sands of history.

During the Middle Ages, and throughout the Renaissance and the Enlightenment, there was a rise of powerful monarchs. Notable figures such as Philip Augustus, Margaret I, Ferdinand the Catholic, Henry VIII, Süleyman the Magnificent, Elizabeth I, Louis the Great, Peter the Great, and Catherine the Great ruled vast empires, controlled great wealth, and created lasting monuments to their rule by building great cities, developing classic architecture, and instituting many cultural advancements that influence our world even today.

Over the past two hundred years, the "profiles" of world leaders have changed again. No longer conquerors or monarchs, the men and women who later stepped onto history's center stage were liberators, revolutionaries, diplomats—and as democracies began to form throughout the world—elected heads of state. Leaders as diverse as Benito Juárez, Giuseppe Garibaldi, Benjamin Disraeli, Woodrow Wilson, Winston Churchill, Franklin D. Roosevelt, Mao Zedong, Golda Meir, and Nelson Mandela helped free and unify their people by throwing off the yoke of colonialism or guided their nations through crises such as wars and economic depressions, truly proving worthy of being called a world leader.

In addition to these people, this book contains biographies of other notable figures, some of whom are harder to categorize, but whose impact on history is undeniable: Siddhārtha Gautama (Buddha), Lorenzo the Magnificent (Lorenzo de' Medici), Napoleon I (Napoléon Bonaparte), Adolf Hitler, Saint John XXIII, Dag Hammarskjöld, and Hirohito.

Ultimately, the one hundred world leaders we have chosen perhaps share at least one common attribute: an inner fortitude that enabled them to rise to greatness—even though some took a darker path and wound up destroying themselves and everything they had built. We believe that each biography contained in this book is fascinating for historical study, and we hope you think so, too.

The second king of the Fourth Dynasty of Egypt's Old Kingdom, pharaoh **KHUFU** is best remembered for building the **Great Pyramid** at Giza to serve as a tomb upon his death.

Historians do not know very much about Khufu because very few written records remain from this period. Historians do know that Khufu succeeded his father, King Snefru, and ruled Egypt with the help of many of his relatives. He most likely had four different wives throughout his life, three of whom were buried in smaller pyramids beside his own.

For years, the history of Khufu's dynasty was known through the writings of the Greek historian **Herodotus**, who described the reign as one of oppression and misery. Khufu's later reputation in Egypt was as a wise ruler, thus contradicting these writings.

Khufu's legacy is for building ancient Egypt's most famous lasting monument, the Great Pyramid at Giza. To create this edifice weighing 5.75 million tons—a masterpiece of technical skill and engineering—approximately 2.3 million blocks of stone were cut, transported, and assembled. It took thousands of workers twenty years to complete the Great Pyramid, which stood 481 feet tall at its base of thirteen acres. It was built at the center of a huge complex of temples, statues, monuments, and lesser tombs for the pharaoh's family.

Herodotus asserts that the cruel tyrant Khufu enslaved people, who toiled in the hot sun to build the pyramid. Later, historians suggested that the construction was a public works project, which kept the rather well-treated agricultural laborers busy and fed when the Nile River was flooding and there was little work to do in the fields.

By the late twentieth century, archaeologists found evidence that a more limited workforce may have occupied the site permanently rather than on a seasonal basis. The excavated laborers' districts included bakeries, storage areas, workshops, and the small tombs of workers and artisans.

Scholars are still not quite sure how the Great Pyramid was built. One theory holds that builders used a long ramp stretching out into the desert. The ramp is guessed to have been continually lengthened and heightened as the pyramid grew higher. Another possible method involved using a circular ramp that rose and wound around the pyramid's exterior as it followed each layer of blocks upward.

Khufu ruled Egypt for more than twenty years. After he died, two of his sons, Redjedef and Khafre, succeeded him.

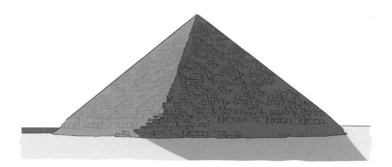

◆ **SARGON** was a Semitic king who built the world's the first real empire in **Mesopotamia**, unifying Sumerian territory with the capital he founded at Akkad.

Much of the historical record about Sargon comes from fragmentary sources and legend, but historians widely believe that he grew up humble. One story says that a gardener found Sargon as an infant in a basket, floating in the river, and brought him up as his own. Sargon's biological father is unknown, and his mother is said to have been a priestess in a town around the middle Euphrates. It follows that Sargon rose to power without the help of influential relatives.

Sargon came from Kish in Sumer, where he earned a high position in service of the court of its ruler, Ur-Zababa. After a military failure by Ur-Zababa, and some confusion about succession, Sargon seized power and built a new capital at Akkad. At the beginning of Sargon's reign, the independent city-states of Sumer had already been defeated and united by **Lugalzagesi** of Uruk (present-day Iraq). In addition to the Sumerian city-states, Lugalzagesi also claimed to rule lands as far west as the Mediterranean, and he had established trade contracts from the Indus Valley to distant Crete.

Sargon first defeated Lugalzagesi at Uruk, and then, in a series of battles, conquered the last of the independent states of Sumer. Subsequently, the charismatic and powerful Akkadian ruler gained control of the Persian Gulf, conquered Susa, the capital city of Elam (present-day Iran), Upper Mesopotamia, and present-day Syria. Thus, his empire stretched from the **Persian Gulf** to the **Mediterranean Sea**. Some later legends claimed that he even extended his conquests into Anatolia (present-day Turkey) and across the sea to Crete.

Sargon's military expertise and his ability to organize a highly centralized government helped the Akkadian ruler enrich his kingdom with trade. Goods were exchanged with the peoples of the Indus Valley, the coastal regions of Oman, the islands and shores of the Persian Gulf, Badakhshān (near the present-day border of Afghanistan and China), the Taurus Mountains, Cappadocia, Crete, and perhaps even Greece.

Probably due to the inability of one ruler to control such a vast empire, rebellions troubled the latter part of Sargon's reign. Two of his sons, Rimush and Manishtushu, succeeded him and further consolidated the empire.

HAMMURABI, king of Babylon, is best remembered for developing the world's first written legal code, a series of laws that governed all aspects of life for **Babylonia**.

Hammurabi was a well-known and respected monarch remembered for bringing "order and righteousness in the land." However, his code was little more than forgotten folklore until 1901, when a French archaeologist excavating in present-day southwestern Iran discovered a seven-foot-high stela, or stone slab, with the Code of Hammurabi carved in cuneiform.

The Code of Hammurabi depicts him as shepherd of his people and a just ruler. The Code covered civil, criminal, and commercial matters. The 282 laws specified conduct—and, where necessary, punishments—in everything ranging from murder to the illegal felling of trees. Penalties for breaking the laws could be severe and were based, for the most part, on the principle of the lex talionis—the punishment fits the crime. Therefore, the Code said that: "If a man put out the eye of another man, his eye shall be put out." Punishments were meted out according to social status, with some violations compensated by silver.

Since the king was also the empire's chief priest, the Code also governed Babylonian religious life. For the first time, laws were published and codified for all to see, and in this manner, the Code was the precursor of modern legal systems applied in most present-day societies.

During his reign, Hammurabi brought Babylon to preeminence in the Mesopotamian world—a reputation it maintained for more than a thousand years. Along with his legal system, he installed a centralized government and formed a standing army. When he came to power, his kingdom was eighty miles long and twenty miles wide, surrounded by much larger states and more powerful rulers. After spending seven years to strengthen his realm from within, Hammurabi ventured to expand his borders. In time, his kingdom stretched as far as the Persian Gulf and to parts of Assyria. Through expansion, he not only added new territory but also acquired necessary raw materials.

Hammurabi also engaged in the traditional activities of an ancient Mesopotamian king: building and restoring temples, city walls, and public buildings; digging canals; and dedicating cult objects to deities in the cities and towns of his realm. His letters show that he personally engaged in the details of implementing these changes.

The last few years of Hammurabi's reign were without major conflicts, but by this time, he was a sick man. When he died around 1750 BCE, his son, Samsuiluna, was already carrying the burden of governing the empire.

◆ The second and greatest king of the Israelites, **DAVID** united Israel and Judah, and established a strong kingdom with Jerusalem as its capital.

The youngest son of Jesse of Bethlehem—and grandson of Boaz and Ruth—David spent his youth tending sheep until he entered King Saul's service as a harpist. At the time, the Israelite's fiercest enemy was the **Philistines**, a prosperous and technologically advanced people, who ruled the Palestinian interior. David became Saul's principal commander and won several military campaigns. He formed a close friendship with Saul's son and heir, Jonathan, and married Saul's daughter, Michal.

After David's many successful forays against the Philistines, Saul became jealous and sought to assassinate the young man. However, David formed an army with Israelites who were dissatisfied with Saul, who soon lost his own life at the hands of the Philistines on Mount Gilboa. His son Jonathan was also slain.

Over the years, David had gained the favor of many Judean elders by protecting them against their enemies. Thus, he was elected king of Judah, not as a rebel against Saul, but as his true successor. He soon gained power over the northern tribes, and eventually took over the rule of Israel. To control both lands, David and his army conquered **Jerusalem**, along a route linking the two kingdoms, and he made the city his capital. He went on to conquer the Philistines and made their land a vassal state.

In Israel's religious tradition of the time, the king mediated between the deity and his people, and he was thought of as both human and divine. In Jerusalem, David based his rule on the ancient cult of Mt. Zion, renaming it the cult of **Yahweh**, by whose power he had triumphed. David then brought the **Ark of the Covenant** to Jerusalem, making it the center of the cult. This rectangular wooden box represented the presence of Yahweh amid the people of Israel. Thus, David was both military and spiritual leader of his people.

David had many wives and concubines, and many of his children caused trouble. One of his sons, Absalom, by his wife Haggith, revolted against his father after David's eldest son raped Absalom's sister and went unpunished. David left the city, returned with his mercenaries, and Absalom was overcome. David also put down a second rebellion led by Sheba, another son. Throughout the remainder of his rule, David faced recurrent wars with the Philistines, but he never suffered a major defeat. When he died, his kingdom stretched from the Euphrates River in the northeast to the Gulf of Aqaba in the southeast.

Upon David's death, his son Solomon, by his wife Bathsheba, succeeded him.

◆ Founder of one of the world's earliest and greatest empires, **CYRUS THE GREAT** came to power by defeating his own grandfather, Astyages, king of Media (present-day Iran) and overlord of the **Persians.**

According to legend, Astyages gave his daughter away in marriage to a Persian prince named Cambyses. From their union, Cyrus was born. Meanwhile, Astyages dreamt that the baby would grow up to overthrow him and ordered Cyrus to be killed. Instead, Astyages's chief adviser gave the baby to a shepherd to raise.

When the outstanding qualities of 10-year-old Cyrus came to the attention of Astyages, the king was persuaded to let the boy live. After Cyrus reached manhood, he gathered the forces of other Persian tribes and revolted against his grandfather. Mindful of the dream, Astyages marched against the rebel, but his army deserted him, and he surrendered to Cyrus in 550 BCE. Cyrus then entered the Median capital of Ecbatana (present-day Hamadan) and took up the throne as king of the Persian Empire.

Two years later, Cyrus went to war against **Croesus**, the king of Lydia (present-day Turkey). The Persian ruler captured Croesus and claimed the fabulous wealth of the kingdom for himself. Cyrus then turned his attention to **Babylon**. Nabonidus, the Babylonian ruler, was an unpopular king. He paid too little attention to the affairs of his kingdom and had alienated the native Babylonian priesthood. Cyrus took advantage of this fact, and the greatest city in the Middle East fell swiftly. In the late summer of 539 BCE, Cyrus marched into Babylon and seized the hands of the statue of **Marduk**, the god of the city, as a signal of his desire to rule as a Babylonian and not as a foreign conqueror. Many of the Babylonians hailed him as the legitimate successor to the throne.

Cyrus's policies toward his subjects were enlightened and tolerant. The Medians had access to important administrative posts, and the Hebrews were freed from their Babylonian captivity and allowed to start rebuilding the Temple at Jerusalem. Generally, Cyrus refrained from interfering with the native customs and religions of the different peoples under his reign.

After the capture of Babylon, Cyrus came to control a vast empire, stretching from the Indus River to the Mediterranean, from the Caucasus region to the Indian Ocean. Through his conquests, the richness of Persian culture was spread to much of the then-developed world.

In 530 BCE, Cyrus tried to repel attacks on the northern section of his empire by the nomadic Massagetai tribes. However, his troops were defeated, and he was killed. Cyrus was buried at Pasargadae (present-day Iran). His son Cambyses II succeeded him.

6 SIDDHĀRTHA GAUTAMA (BUDDHA)

c. 563–483 BCE

The founder of **Buddhism**, **SIDDHĀRTHA GAUTAMA** is one of the most significant leaders in the history of world religions. For more than two thousand years, Buddhism has played a central role in the spiritual, cultural, and social life of millions of people around the world.

Born around 563 BCE, the son of a local ruler in northern India, Siddhārtha was raised in the luxury of his father's realm. At age sixteen, he married a neighboring princess, and they became the parents of at least one child. As he grew older, Siddhārtha continued to be shielded from life's problems. Only four times did he leave the palace for brief periods, and each time, he encountered pain. He saw an old man, a sick man, a dead man, and a man committed to a religious life. These encounters with life's hardships are known to Buddhists today as the **Four Meetings**. They transformed Siddhārtha's life, and after these experiences, he sought an answer to the universal problem of suffering.

Despite his comfortable existence, Siddhārtha became discontented. At the age of twenty-nine, against his family's wishes, he left the palace, renounced his privileged existence, and began a six-year-long spiritual quest. He placed himself under the spiritual guidance of two recluses and followed their meditative discipline. Disappointed with their methods, he eventually left and joined the Jains, an austere group that did not believe in harming any living thing. However, after five years of practicing Jainism, Siddhārtha realized that he still hadn't found the answers he longed for.

At around the age of thirty-five, Siddhārtha journeyed to Bodh-Gaya in northeast India. He rested under a fig tree, letting his mind mull over his previous experiences. After his long meditation, Siddhārtha had a spiritual awakening, or a full "enlightenment." He began to teach what he had learned, and soon many followers flocked to him. As his teachings spread, he became known as "Buddha, the Enlightened One."

Buddha's teachings focus on the **Four Noble Truths**. The first premise is that all existence is suffering, and there is no escape from the pain of human existence. Second, the cause of suffering comes from desire. Third, the release from suffering comes when desire ceases. Fourth, the way to cease suffering is through the **Eightfold Path**.

The Eightfold Path consists of right understanding, right thoughts, right speech, right action, right livelihood, right effort, right mindfulness, and right concentration. By following this correct path, or dharma, the soul can achieve a state of **Nirvana**, which is the perfect final state of peace.

For the next forty-five years, Buddha taught his beliefs to many followers, who in turn carried on the teachings. Buddhism became one of the world's major religions.

Great-grandson of Cyrus the Great (see no. 5), the founder of the Persian Empire, **XERXES I** tried to complete a job his father, Darius I, had left unfinished, which was the conquest of **Greece**.

Before Darius died in 486 BCE, he had succeeded in expanding the empire by consolidating Persian rule over Egypt. However, his eventual goal of conquering the Greek city-states was thwarted when the outnumbered but better trained Greeks defeated him at the Battle of Marathon in 490 BCE.

Ten years later, Xerxes I set about accomplishing what his father had been unable to do. First, Xerxes I suppressed a revolt in Egypt, where a usurper had been governing for two years. Xerxes I left one of his brothers, Achaemenes, in charge of the Egyptians, who were burdened by new taxes and endured materials being confiscated from their temples.

Around 482 BCE, a major revolt in Babylonia temporarily halted Xerxes I's plans to finish the invasion into Greece. As in Egypt, Xerxes I suppressed this uprising with a heavy hand, destroying the great ziggurat (pyramidal temple) and the temple of Marduk.

Finally, in 481 BCE, Xerxes I turned his attention to Greece. He led a combined land and sea invasion, with estimated forces of three hundred thousand men. The invaders took northern Greece in the summer of 480 BCE, and proceeded south, toward the narrow mountain pass at **Thermopylae**. There some three hundred Spartan warriors fought a valiant battle, delaying the Persian advance and inflicting heavy losses on the invaders before they finally broke through. The Persian land forces then marched on to Athens, taking the city and burning the Acropolis.

On the sea, the Persians had lost many ships because of stormy weather, but they still had a more than two-to-one advantage when they met the Greeks in the narrow straits of **Salamis**. Still, the Greeks emerged victorious, strategically setting fire to many Persian vessels and outmaneuvering the rest in the narrow waterways that they knew so well.

Xerxes I withdrew from Athens and Greece and returned home where he regrouped over the winter and returned the following spring to the **Plain of Plataea**. Once again, the outnumbered Greeks defeated the larger and more powerful Persian forces, extinguishing any hopes Xerxes I had of conquering Greece.

Although Xerxes I never succeeded in his conquest of Greece, the Persian Empire reached its height under his reign and progressively declined thereafter. In 465 BCE, Xerxes I was assassinated in a palace plot by a minister named **Artabanus**, who planned to take over the throne. Artabanus deceived Xerxes I's son, Artaxerxes, into thinking his brother Darius had killed their father, but when Artaxerxes learned the truth, he killed Artabanus and ascended the throne.

◆ Politician, political leader, and military leader, **PERICLES** dominated the political and intellectual life of democratic **Athens** when that city-state was at the height of its imperial power and cultural greatness.

Born around 495 BCE, Pericles was a descendant of a wealthy family, and enjoyed a progressive education. He entered politics around 469 BCE. A great orator, he became a leader in the Athenian democracy movement, and rose to become the most powerful ruler in Athens. Under his leadership, Athens achieved massive political and cultural progress.

Pericles was a patron of the arts, and during this period, Athenian architecture and sculpture reached their greatest level of development. Numerous public buildings were constructed, including such marvels as the **Parthenon**; literature and fine art flourished as never before; and dramatic festivals were held that even the poorer residents could attend. Athens became the most magnificent city of the ancient world.

Under Pericles, Athens also became a strong military power. He built the Athenian fleet into one of the greatest in the world, and he led its army into many battles, attacking Delphi and putting down revolts in Euboea and Samos. Politically, he introduced a truly democratic system in which free citizens held public office. He also initiated salaries for civil servants and allowances for the poor.

Around 450 BCE, Pericles met a woman named **Aspasia**, who had gone to Athens and opened a school of rhetoric and philosophy. Many of the daughters and wives of Athenian leaders studied with her, and she soon became widely known. Pericles fell in love her and divorced his wife. Although he was forbidden to marry Aspasia because she was a foreigner, they made a home and a life together.

Despite his many successes, Pericles was unable to put an end to the many wars that had plagued Athens and the other Greek city-states. In 431 BCE, rival city-state Sparta broke a peace treaty and declared war on Athens. This action set off three decades of conflict known as the **Peloponnesian War**.

The war began well for Athens, and Pericles was hailed for his military strategy. When the Spartans invaded, Pericles persuaded the Athenians to abandon the countryside, retreat within the city's walls, and to rely on their fleet. Then, in the war's second year, a plague ravaged the city. Pericles was attacked by his enemies and was briefly deposed from leadership. He was soon reelected with more powers, but shortly after that, the plague claimed Pericles as one of its victims.

After his death, the Athenian state gradually declined due to the continuing war with Sparta and the lack of a suitable replacement for the dynamic leadership of Pericles.

PTOLEMY I SOTER, a Macedonian general who fought alongside **Alexander the Great**, became the ruler of **Egypt** and the founder of the Ptolemaic dynasty, which lasted for nearly three centuries.

Ptolemy I Soter was the son of nobleman Lagus and Arsinoe, who was related to the Macedonian Argead dynasty and had formerly been a concubine of Alexander's father, Philip II. In his youth, Ptolemy I Soter served as a page for the Macedonian royal court, where he became closely associated with the young crown prince, Alexander. After Alexander's ascension to the throne in 336 BCE, Ptolemy I Soter joined the king's bodyguard.

Before long, Ptolemy I Soter had become one of Alexander's most trusted generals, playing a major role in Alexander's campaigns in now Afghanistan and India around 327–326 BCE. The young king decorated Ptolemy I Soter several times for his deeds and married him to the Persian Aracama at a mass wedding at Susa. The wedding sealed Alexander's policy of merging the Macedonian and Persian populations. Artacama was one of Ptolemy I Soter's four wives.

After Alexander's death in 323 BCE, his vast empire was divided up among several of his generals. Ptolemy I Soter became *satrap*, or governor, of Egypt. During his reign, he developed administrative, financial, and commercial infrastructures. He also established a glorious new capital at Alexandria, which would become the greatest city in the world. Its museum and grand library attracted scholars from far and wide. Besides being a patron of the arts and sciences, Ptolemy I Soter was a writer. In the last few years of his life, he wrote a generally reliable history of Alexander the Great's campaigns.

Throughout his lengthy reign, Ptolemy I Soter waged many wars against foreign rulers to both solidify his hold on Egypt and expand his territory. Despite these wars, Ptolemy I Soter governed well, and under his rule, Egypt became a formidable power. By the time he died, he controlled Cyprus, Palestine, and many cities in the **Aegean** and **Asia Minor** regions. During the last fifteen years of his reign, Ptolemy I Soter turned to securing and expanding his empire through alliances and marriages rather than through warfare.

As he neared the end of his life, Ptolemy I Soter made provisions for a successor. In 290 BCE, his wife Berenice became queen of Egypt, and in 285 BCE, his younger son Ptolemy II Philadelphus, who was born in 308 BCE, became co-regent and successor. The provision for the succession made for a peaceful transition when Ptolemy I Soter died in the winter of 283 BCE. After his death, the Egyptians proclaimed him a god.

The last of the Ptolemaic rulers was Cleopatra VII, paramour of Julius Caesar and Marc Anthony.

The greatest conqueror of the ancient world, **ALEXANDER THE GREAT** ruled a vast empire that straddled both Europe and Asia and disseminated the Greek language and culture over much of the known world.

This remarkable leader was born at Pella in **Macedonia**. He was the son of King Philip II and Olympias, daughter of the king of Epirus. Greek philosopher Aristotle tutored Alexander from thirteen to sixteen. Alexander showed a keen mind, and his teacher inspired his interest in philosophy, medicine, and science.

Alexander's parents divorced, and his future became uncertain after he sided with his mother in a dispute with his father. As a result, he was forced to flee with her to Epirus. Shortly afterward, father and son reconciled, and Alexander returned to his home. When Philip was assassinated in 336 BCE, the military proclaimed Alexander as successor, who then assumed the kingship.

After seeking revenge against those he believed were responsible for his father's murder, Alexander marched southward and brought a wavering Thessaly under control. When a false rumor of his death precipitated a revolt among Theban democrats, Alexander demanded their surrender. When they refused, he entered Thebes and razed it to the ground, sparing only temples and the poet Pindar's house. Alexander's forces slaughtered six thousand Thebans and sold the survivors into slavery.

One major goal Alexander had was to continue his father's campaign to punish the **Persians** for Xerxes I's invasion of Greece nearly 150 years earlier. In 333 BCE, Alexander fought a major battle against **Darius III**, king of the Persians, at Issus (modern-day Turkey). Alexander used the mobility of his troops to confuse and defeat the much larger Persian army.

Alexander then marched into **Egypt** where the people welcomed him without resistance, and the high priests declared him a god. In 331 BCE, in a final attempt to destroy Darius and his entire army, Alexander won a second major battle against the much larger Persian army at Arabela. Darius escaped but was later killed by one of his own generals. The victorious Alexander marched into the Persian capital, Persepolis, and took it. He thereafter ruled the Persian Empire in cooperation with Persian nobility, some of whom he appointed as governors.

Alexander spent the next several years trying to spread Greek culture to all reaches of his growing empire because he wanted the Greeks, Persians, and Macedonians to become one ethnic group.

Alexander marched his army all the way to the Indus River, where he fought a battle against Indian troops and their elephants. Finally, in 326 BCE, his weary forces demanded to return home. On the journey back, Alexander died in Babylon in 323 BCE. He was buried in **Alexandria**, Egypt, a city he had founded.

LIU BANG was the founder and first emperor of the **Han** dynasty, which lasted four hundred years, and under which the Chinese imperial system assumed most of the characteristics it would keep until the twentieth century.

Born into a peasant family, Liu Bang was a police officer under the Jin dynasty. In 210 BCE, after the death of the Jin emperor Qin Shi Huang, who had been the first to unify China, Liu joined the rebels under the leadership of **Hsiang Yii**. Hsiang was a warlord who tried to restore the feudal system, reinstating many of the former nobles and dividing the land among his generals. Since Liu Bang was an important leader, he received control of the kingdom of Han in West China (present-day Sichuan and southern Shaanxi provinces).

By 206 BCE, Hsiang and Liu turned against each other. Liu's peasant shrewdness helped lead him to victory over his militarily brilliant but politically naive rival. The civil war ended in 202 BCE, when Hsiang Yii took his own life, rather than surrender. Liu then became ruler of China, taking the name of Han Gaozu, or "Exulted Emperor of Han." He then began the lengthy process of reunifying China.

In domestic affairs, Liu instituted a system of laissez-faire politics. The rulers in the populous eastern part of the empire were sons of the emperor and marquisates, or local aristocratic supporters of the throne who collected taxes in return for land. In the western half, fourteen commanderies ruled. These officials, rather than the emperor, initiated most policy proposals, which Gaozu then discussed with his ministerial advisers before making a decision.

Gaozu was a coarse man who disdained education. Nevertheless, he was both pragmatic and flexible, recognizing the need for

the presence of educated men at court. He showed particular concern for reviving the rural economy and alleviating the tax burden of the peasants and their conscription as laborers. His policies led to population growth, expansion of the economy, and a flourishing culture.

In foreign affairs, Gaozu used a skillful combination of diplomacy and force. To gain the support of otherwise belligerent nomad chieftains, he offered gifts, particularly that of silk and the hand of a Han daughter in marriage.

Although Gaozu intensely disliked the teachings of the once popular **Confucius** and philosophers in general, his successors would incorporate Confucianism into their governments as they continued the process of consolidating and expanding the empire. While Gaozu's rule was short, it nevertheless set the stage for the Han dynasty to flourish and set up subsequent Han rulers to establish the **Mandarin** social and political system, which survived as the basis of Chinese society right up until the mid-twentieth century and the introduction of communism.

A brilliant military leader and the first sole ruler of the **Roman Empire, JULIUS CAESAR** expanded the power and glory of Rome before being betrayed and ultimately destroyed by his former supporters.

Gaius Julius Caesar was born into a patrician family. After joining the Roman army and serving in Asia, Caesar returned to Rome, entered politics, and rose quickly to powerful positions. He became pontifex maximus, or high priest, in 63 BCE as part of a deal with the general **Pompey** (Caesar's son-in-law), and **Crassus**, a banker with whom he formed the so-called first triumvirate, or a ruling group of three.

In 59 BCE, Caesar became governor of southern Gaul (present-day France); he soon set out on a military campaign to enhance his own power and extend the glory of Rome. He subjugated the rest of Gaul, conquered Helvetii (present-day Switzerland), Belgica (present-day Belgium), crossed the River Rhine to fight the German tribes, and made two expeditions to Britain.

Caesar's brilliance as a commander inspired great loyalty among his soldiers. His acumen as a general alarmed Roman aristocrats, who feared he might take control of Rome.

The Senate, induced by Pompey—his enemy and rival—ordered him back to Rome, but without his army. Caesar defied the order and led his troops across the **Rubicon**, a small river that separated his province in Gaul from Italy. Civil war ensued.

Caesar took Rome and then pursued the fleeing Pompey to Greece, where Caesar defeated him at the **Battle of Pharsalus**, in 48 BCE. Caesar then campaigned in Asia Minor, Egypt, Africa, and Spain, before returning to Rome in 45 BCE.

After Caesar's conquest in Rome, the Senate appointed him dictator of Rome. After the hostilities ceased, he pardoned all his surviving enemies. His wide-ranging program of reform included the institution of the Julian calendar, the lowering of taxes, the extension of citizenship to more provincials, and initiating a public works program to provide employment and to beautify the city.

However, Caesar flaunted his ascendancy and ignored Rome's republican traditions. Some of his enemies alleged that he wanted to be king, which was anathema to Romans. A politician named **Cassius** conspired with a former colleague and friend of Caesar's named **Marcus Brutus** to assassinate the leader. As Caesar entered the Roman Senate on March 15, 44 BCE, he was stabbed to death.

Caesar's murder plunged Rome into yet another civil war, but eventually Caesar's chosen successor, his great-nephew **Gaius Octavius**, emerged victorious and became the first emperor of the Roman Empire. Julius Caesar was later deified, and a temple was dedicated to his worship in the Roman Forum.

As emperor of the Roman Empire, **CONSTANTINE** changed the course of history by ending centuries of Christian persecution and making **Christianity** the empire's official religion.

Constantine was the son of a Roman army officer, Flavius Valerius Constantius, and Helena of Bithynia, his wife or concubine for nineteen years. By the early fourth century, the Roman Empire had become divided. One ruler led the Western Empire (Italy, Gaul, Britain, and Spain), while another controlled the Eastern Empire (Greece, Syria, Asia Minor and Egypt). In 305, Constantius became the emperor of the **Western Empire** until he died the next year, and the army proclaimed Constantine the new emperor.

However, a period of unrest ensued as several contenders competed for power, and Constantine had to wage several battles to retain control. By 312, he had defeated all his rivals, with the exception of his brother-in-law, **Maxentius**. Just before a crucial battle with Maxentius at the Milvian Bridge near Rome, Constantine supposedly saw a vision in the sky with the sign of the cross as a battle standard. When he killed Maxentius and won the battle, Constantine took it as a sign of approval. After his victory, he declared himself a Christian.

In 313, Constantine had a meeting with Licinius, emperor of the Eastern Empire. Out of the meeting came Constantine's proclamation, the **Edict of Milan**, which gave equal rights to people of all religions and ended the persecutions of Christians.

Constantine and Licinius fought in 314 over mutually owned territories. The victorious Constantine acquired Illyricum (on the East Adriatic coast), Pannonia (around present-day Hungary), and Greece, and peace was restored. However, in 323, serious problems arose once more. Constantine won a major battle at Adrianople (present-day Greece) and emerged as the sole ruler of the full empire.

Constantine reunited the empire under his rule. He reorganized the army, recruiting more cavalry troops and creating a more mobile force, which enabled the empire to better defend itself against its enemies.

Constantine also created a new imperial capital at **Constantinople** (present-day Istanbul). It was chosen because of its strategic proximity to the Danube and Euphrates frontiers, and the economic importance of the harbor.

As a committed Christian, Constantine also sought to settle a major dispute over doctrine between the eastern and western factions of the church.

In 325, he convened the Council of Nicaea, a conference of 220 bishops representing both sides. The meeting resulted in the **Nicene Creed**, which set out the basic Christian beliefs upon which both sides could agree. Constantine then established Christianity as the official state religion.

Constantine was baptized a Christian a few weeks before he died in May 337. His burial site immediately became a place of pilgrimage.

As warlord and leader of the **Visigoths, ALARIC** led the army that sacked Rome in 410, an event that symbolized the fall of the Western Roman Empire.

Alaric was born on the island of Peuce, located at the mouth of the Danube River in present-day Romania. Noble by birth, he commanded the Gothic (Germanic) troops in the Roman army and helped defeat the Western usurper Emperor Eugenius in 394. Shortly after the death of Emperor Theodosius I the following year, Alaric left the army, and the Visigoth tribe elected him as their chief.

In 390, complaining that his tribe had not been given their promised subsidies, Alaric marched his forces against the Eastern Roman Empire, which was centered at Constantinople. His advance was halted by Roman forces under the command of **Flavius Stilicho**.

In 395, Alaric moved southward into Greece, where he sacked Piraeus, and ravaged the cities of Corinth, Megara, Argos, and Sparta. The Eastern Emperor Arcadius finally placated the Visigoths in 397 with a bribe. He then appointed Alaric as governor of **Illyricum**.

In 401, Alaric turned his attention to the Western Empire and invaded Italy, but once again, he was thwarted by Stilicho. Roman troops defeated Alaric in 402 at Pollentia and forced the Visigoths to withdraw from the Italian peninsula. Alaric invaded a second time, and his efforts once more met defeat. At this time, he entered into a peace treaty with Stilicho. Despite his losses, Alaric eventually convinced the Senate at Rome to pay a large subsidy to his tribe.

After Emperor **Honorius** had Stilicho executed in August 408, Alaric asked the emperor for land and supplies, a request he refused. The Visigothic chieftain then laid siege to Rome until the Senate agreed to another subsidy and assistance in his negotiations with Honorius. The emperor remained intransigent, however, and in 409, Alaric again surrounded Rome. He lifted his blockade only after proclaiming his own man, Attalus, as emperor. Attalus then appointed Alaric commander-in-chief of the Roman forces.

After Alaric deposed Attalus in the summer of 410, the Visigoths besieged Rome for the third time. When Alaric's allies within Rome opened the gates to him, his troops occupied the city—which had not been captured by a foreign enemy for nearly eight hundred years. The Visigoths plundered the city and ravaged buildings and monuments for three days.

Alaric then tried to follow through with his plan to occupy Sicily and Africa, but on the way to those lands, a storm destroyed his fleet. He died suddenly just a few months after the assault on Rome. Legend says that he was buried at a secret location on the Busento River.

A ruthless but natural leader of fighting men, **ATTILA** led his warriors in a series of bloody campaigns that nearly destroyed the foundation of Western Christendom.

The Huns were a warlike, nomadic people from **Central Asia** who swept into the Black Sea and Danube River regions around 370. Their arrival displaced many of the Visigothic and Ostrogothic tribes—people who posed less of a threat to the Romans than the Huns.

In 433, Attila and his brother Bleda inherited the leadership of the tribe from their uncle. The brothers jointly ruled a chiefdom that stretched from the Alps and the Baltic in the west to the Caspian Sea in the east. At the time, the Huns were receiving an annual tribute of seven hundred pounds of gold from the Eastern Roman Empire in Constantinople as a price for peace.

While the Vandals in northern Africa were threatening Egypt—the granary for the Middle East—and also the supply lines to Constantinople, Attila took advantage of the situation. He ignored the truce between the Huns and the Eastern Empire and moved against Roman forts on the north bank of the Danube in 440. He attacked and destroyed towns and cities as far south as present-day Sofia, Bulgaria. Attila's invasion won concessions from the emperor; the annual tribute was raised to two thousand one hundred pounds of gold.

Around 445, Attila murdered his brother Bleda, and became ruler of the Huns.

In 451, this "Scourge of God" decided to attack the Western Roman Empire, invading Gaul with an enormous army composed of Huns and various other tribespeople. At the Battle of Chalons, Attila met his only defeat, at the hands of combined Roman, Frankish, and Visigoth forces. While the Visigoth king Theodoric was killed in the fierce fighting, the Huns and their allies suffered heavy losses.

After withdrawing from Gaul, Attila then turned on Italy, where his forces destroyed several northern towns and occupied Milan. With his army set to march on Rome, Pope Leo I came north and met with Attila, who had high regard for spiritual people. After their conversation, Attila decided to leave Italy. Pope Leo I became the champion of Christianity, but some historians believe that the famine and pestilence raging in Italy would have compelled the Huns to leave anyway.

In 453, as he recrossed the Alps, Attila died during the evening of his marriage to a young Hunnite woman. A legend says that after a heavy feast and excessive drinking, he suffered a bloody nose and drowned in his own blood.

Shortly after his death, the Huns broke into smaller groups and their influence declined.

The reign of **THEODORIC**, king of the **Ostrogoths** and founder of the Ostrogothic Kingdom in Italy, brought about the beginnings of the synthesis of Roman and German cultures.

Theodoric was born in the Roman province of Pannonia (present-day Hungary). Sent as a hostage to Constantinople at the age of eight, he was educated in Greco-Roman cultural values and remained there until he was seventeen. Elected king in 471 after his father's death, Theodoric became involved in intrigues both against and with the Byzantine Emperor Zeno, who finally, in the late 480s, sent Theodoric on a conquest to Italy to be rid of him.

In 493, after a three-year siege of **Ravenna**, Theodoric forced the surrender of Odoacer, the German leader who had deposed the last Roman emperor, Romulus Augustulus. Theodoric had Odoacer killed, and then became ruler of Italy with Ravenna as his capital. Such an invasion promised a homeland for Theodoric's wandering people. At its greatest size, his empire included Italy, Sicily, Dalmatia, and parts of Germany.

Though the Romans and the Germanic peoples differed in creed, race, and culture, Theodoric managed to hold together his kingdom peacefully during his thirty-three-year reign. He maintained law and order, preserved Roman legal institutions, and appointed Roman officials to civil service jobs, while retaining a Gothic army. He zealously encouraged trade and skilled crafts.

Improvements were made in agriculture and public works.

He also used religious tolerance and alliances to consolidate his power. Though Theodoric was an **Arian Christian** which means he believed Jesus was not divine, he tolerated all other Christian sects and was a protector of the Jews. As marriage alliances were important in the politics of the time, Theodoric aligned himself through marriage to Clovis I, the great Frankish king, by marrying the king's sister. Nevertheless, Clovis I desired to rule all the Goths, and Theodoric was forced into intermittent warfare with the Franks. He also engineered alliances with the Visigoths, the Vandals, and the Burgundians.

One of the acts that Theodoric most bitterly regretted was hastily ordering the brutal execution of **Boethius**, who was known as "the last of the Romans." Boethius was a philosopher and government official who tried to rescue the intellectual heritage of the ancient Greeks and Romans through translations of the works of Aristotle and others. Boethius was imprisoned and executed without a trial for an alleged plot against the throne.

A quarrel between his Roman subjects and Pope John I over the edicts of Emperor Justin I against Arianism marred the end of Theodoric's reign. After his death, the Emperor **Justinian I** (see no. 17) ordered the Ostrogoths removed from Italy, and his forces drove them across the Alps to an unknown end.

During his nearly forty-year reign, Emperor **JUSTINIAN I** strengthened and enlarged the **Byzantine Empire**, and he is remembered for codifying all existing Roman laws.

Born into a family of peasants in present-day Turkey, Justinian I was brought to Constantinople by his uncle, Justin I, who commanded the imperial bodyguard of the Byzantine Emperor Leo I at the time. As a young man, Justinian I was well educated in Greek and Latin and then took up a military career. When his uncle became emperor, Justinian I served as his adviser. Emperor Justin I legally adopted his nephew, marking him as heir and successor to the throne.

In 525, Justinian I married **Theodora**, a reputed beauty and former actress who became his invaluable ally and adviser for the rest of his life. When Justin I died in 527, Justinian I became emperor, and Theodora empress. Soon after, Justinian I made major administrative changes and increased state revenue at the expense of his subjects.

The burden of Justinian I's taxation policies, and the strong opposition of a dissident Christian sect, produced the widespread **Nika** riots in Constantinople in 532. With much of the city burning and parts of his palace destroyed, Justinian I wanted to flee. Empress Theodora, however, persuaded him to stand his ground. His forces rallied, and before it was over, the rebellion had been put down at the cost of more than thirty thousand lives. With his power firmly established, Justinian I now turned his attention to the West.

The emperor considered it his duty to regain provinces previously lost to the empire. During the 530s and 540s, he dispatched his generals to recover lands in Africa from the Vandals and in Italy from the Ostrogoths. By 563, he reigned over the entire Roman Empire formerly ruled by Constantine the Great (see no. 13) except for Britain, Gaul, and parts of Spain.

Justinian I's greatest accomplishments were in his work as a codifier and legislator. Under his direction, the jurist Tribonian and his staff completed a ten-year compilation of all existing Roman law. It gave unity to the centralized state and greatly influenced all subsequent legal history.

Justinian I also instituted a large-scale program of public works, erecting a great number of buildings in many cities. Among his feats was the building of the **Hagia Sophia**, the supreme pinnacle of Byzantine art, which stands today as a museum in Istanbul.

Throughout his reign, Justinian I not only relied on the counsel of Empress Theodora, but he also allowed her to have widespread influence. She was devoted to social justice, particularly for women and children. During her reign, divorced women gained more rights, and children could not be sold to pay off their parents' debt.

After Justinian's death in 565, his nephew Justin II succeeded him.

AL-MANṢŪR firmly established the Islamic **'Abbāsid** caliphate, a dynasty that ruled from Spain to Baghdad (present-day Iraq) during the height of Arab civilization.

Al-Manṣūr was born in Al-Ḥumaymah, the home of the 'Abbāsid family after emigrating from the Hejaz in 687–688. The family claimed they were descendants of 'Abbās, the uncle of **Muḥammad**, the founder of Islam. Therefore, they asserted, they were the true heirs to his rule and the true leaders of the Arab nations.

With this claim, the 'Abbāsids led a coalition of Persians and Iraqis in a revolution that toppled the first Islamic rulers, the **Umayyads**, in 750. Abū al-'Abbās al-Saffāḥ, al-Manṣūr's brother, became the first 'Abbāsid caliph, or ruler. When he died in 754, al-Manṣūr undertook the task of establishing the 'Abbāsid dynasty.

Numerous revolts by ambitious army commanders threatened al-Manṣūr's caliphate. The most serious was the revolt in 754 led by al-Manṣūr's uncle, 'Abd Allāh, the governor of Syria, who thought he had a stronger right to rule the caliphate than his nephew. The rebellion was only thwarted with the help of Abū Muslim, one of the chief organizers of the revolt against the Umayyads.

Al-Manṣūr was largely responsible for changing the course of history for the 'Abbāsids. While his brother was still caliph, al-Manṣūr was involved in the murder of several leading personalities in the movement that brought the caliphate to power. Upon becoming caliph himself, one of al-Manṣūr's first acts was to bring about the death of Abū Muslim, the man who had helped him retain power. These acts served both to remove potential rivals and to dissociate the 'Abbāsids from their supporters, who were seen as extremists.

During al-Manṣūr's reign, force was also used to repulse foreign invasions from the Byzantines (758), annex new territory in Tabaristan (759), and put down revolts in Iraq and Medina (762). However, the crowning accomplishment of al-Manṣūr's reign, and his lasting legacy, was the construction of the city of **Baghdad** in 762.

The city was built in the form of a circle around the Great Mosque and the caliph's palace—symbolizing the close association of religious and political power. The new capital was also built to house the rapidly growing bureaucracy that Iranian-influenced al-Manṣūr developed to provide a stable basis for 'Abbāsid rule.

Al-Manṣūr lived a life of simplicity. He was a lover of poetry and a patron of the arts, and he encouraged the translation of Greek and Latin texts into Arabic. He died in 775 on his way to **Mecca** for a pilgrimage and was buried near the holy city.

The reign of **CHARLEMAGNE**, the greatest European ruler of the **Middle Ages**, represented the merging of German, Christian, and Roman traditions—the essential characteristics of medieval civilization.

Born in Aachen in present-day Germany, Charlemagne (French for "Charles the Great") was the grandson of Charles Martel, who was famous for halting Arab expansion into Europe at the Battle of Poitiers in 732. In 768, upon the death of his father Pippin III, Charlemagne inherited the northern half of the Frankish kingdom, and his brother Carolman inherited the southern half. When Carolman died in 771, Charlemagne became sole ruler of both regions.

From the 770s through the 790s, Charlemagne fought many battles against various enemies and succeeded in extending his father's kingdom to eventually include all of continental Europe except Spain, Scandinavia, southern Italy, and the Slavic fringes of the east. Peaceful relations with eastern Muslims and the Byzantine Empire were maintained through embassies and gifts.

Charlemagne ruled his vast empire with the cooperation of noble families who received lands and spoils for their help. He appointed counts and military governors to rule various parts of his realm; he also sent out royal messengers, usually one nobleman and one churchman, on annual journeys to supervise the execution of his laws and to keep an eye on other officials.

By the end of the eighth century, Charlemagne had established a royal palace in Aachen and had become very wealthy. His long-held desire had always been to rule an empire as vast as the old Roman Empire, and at the same time, the Roman Catholic pope sought a single monarch who would rule Europe and protect and serve Christendom. As a result, Charlemagne found himself in Rome on Christmas Day in 800 being crowned **"Emperor of the Romans"** by Pope Leo III. For the next fourteen years, Charlemagne would control more land and people than any European leader since the fall of the Roman Empire more than three hundred years before.

Though a crude and rough man, Charlemagne was a patron of literature, science, and the arts. Among the prominent scholars in his court was **Alcuin of York**, leader of the palace school. These scholars helped create the "**Carolingian Renaissance**," during which knowledge of Latin was renewed, and books were copied using the "Carolingian minuscule"—the first script to use upper- and lowercase letters, punctuation, and word spaces.

Charlemagne crowned his only surviving son, Louis I, his co-emperor and sole successor of Aachen in 813. A few months later, the old king died. Although his empire survived him by only one generation, he had established a common intellectual, religious, and political tradition on which later centuries would draw.

ALFRED THE GREAT founded the English navy and repelled countless Danish invasions to keep his homeland free and at the center of **Anglo-Saxon** law and tradition.

Alfred's birthplace was Wessex, a small and independent state of south England. At his birth, it was thought unlikely that Alfred would ever rise to become king because he had three older brothers in line for the crown of their father, Aethelwulft, king of the West Saxons. However, all three had short lives and reigns, and Alfred eventually became king.

The greatest danger for the Anglo-Saxon people at that time was the raids of their lands by the **Danish**. In 870, the Danes threatened the entire Anglo-Saxon kingdom, consisting of Wessex, Mercia, Northumberland, and East Anglia. Alfred aided his king brother, Aethelred I, in commanding the forces of Wessex. At the **Battle of Ashdown** in 871, they defeated the Danish army, but their victory proved temporary and further defeats followed. When Ethelred was slain in battle later in 871, Alfred became king.

In 868, Alfred had married Ealswith, a descendant of Mercian royalty. As king, he forged good relations with the other Anglo-Saxon kingdoms. He also built new forts in Wessex, strengthened older ones, and built the first English ships in preparation for more battles with the Danes.

In 876, the ceasefire ended, and Danish leader **Guthrum** brought his army into Wessex, capturing many towns and causing Alfred to flee to a small fort in the marshes. However, from there, Alfred was able to gather his forces, and two years later, they won a great victory at the **Battle of Edington**. The Danes were baptized Christian upon surrendering, and the Treaty of Wedmore was signed, bringing peace. The Danish King Guthrum honored the treaty until his death in 891. During the remainder of Alfred's reign, he quashed subsequent Danish invasions—skillfully utilizing the navy he had built—until the Danes were forced to give up all hopes of conquering Wessex.

Alfred was a leader in government as well as in war. He organized the finances of the realm and the services due from his thanes, or noble followers. King Alfred founded the civil structure of England, dividing the lands into shires, hundreds, and tithings. He also established a legal code based on existing systems of his predecessors.

A religiously devout and pragmatic man, Alfred recognized the general deterioration in learning and religion caused by the Danish destruction of monasteries. He arranged for and took part in the translation of books from Latin into English.

He died in 899 and was buried in Winchester, the resting place of the West Saxon royal family. His son Edward succeeded him.

A dominant figure in early medieval Europe, **OTTO THE GREAT** established a strong kingship in Germany and founded the **Holy Roman Empire**.

Otto I was the son of King Henry I of Saxony, who was known as "Henry the Fowler." Otto was not formally educated, but in his early years, he received trained in hunting, horsemanship, and the use of arms. In 930, he married Edith, daughter of the English King Edward the Elder.

Although he was called king, Otto's father was actually one of five German dukes of equal power who ruled Saxony, Franconia, Swabia, Bavaria, and Lorraine. Henry nominated Otto to succeed him, and in 936, a month after Henry's death, the German dukes elected Otto his successor.

Otto was determined to turn Germany into an empire. He did away with the independent duchy of Franconia; taking it for himself by cooperating with the Christian Church, he was further able to consolidate his power. He treated the German bishops as if they were counts or dukes, giving them land and titles. In return, they owed allegiance to him, and provided him with knights and soldiers in times of war.

Within the first three years of his rule, Otto was faced with threats from enemies both foreign and domestic, including some from his own family members. After he put down numerous uprisings, Otto then enjoyed twelve years of relative peace. By 950, he managed to bind all five independent German duchies to his crown. Though members of his family ruled over the them, Otto always kept a close eye on his empire.

After 950, the greatest external threat to Otto's empire came from the **Magyars**, a fierce warrior tribe from present-day Hungary. They invaded Germany in 954, ravaging the towns and countryside and murdering the citizens. In 955, Otto soundly defeated the Magyars at the **Battle of Lechfeld** near Augsburg. This victory permanently ended the invasions from the east and earned Otto the title "Otto the Great."

His next venture concerned Rome. Otto cultivated good relations with the papacy, and in 962, Pope **John XII** crowned him Holy Roman emperor, a title that had previously only gone to descendants of Charlemagne (see no. 19). But when Otto made several campaigns into Italy to acquire new lands, the pope turned against him. Otto used his influence in Italy to have the pope deposed and replaced him with his own candidate, who became Pope **Leo VIII**.

As Otto's kingdom expanded, the resultant flowering of culture, referred to as the **Ottonian Renaissance**, helped foster advances in learning and in the arts. When Otto I died in 973, he left behind a united German Empire.

In the space of a generation, **STEPHEN I** went from being a pagan tribal leader to a **Christian** king of a powerful nation.

Stephen I was a member of the **Árpád** dynasty, which came to rule the **Magyar** tribe in present-day Hungary around the end of the ninth century. Son of the Magyar chieftain Geza, Stephen I married Gisela, daughter of Duke Henry II of Bavaria (present-day Germany) in 996. When Geza died the next year, the young man became leader of the Magyars.

Stephen I followed his father's attempts to Christianize his people, but he took a more direct approach. The young king asked Pope Sylvester II to baptize him and crown him king of Hungary, and according to tradition, Stephen I was crowned king on Christmas Day in 1001. With this action, Hungary entered the spiritual community of the Western world, and at the same time, it reduced the possibility of the Holy Roman emperor assuming the role of feudal lord over Hungary and making the Hungarian ruler his vassal. With the exception of one invasion by Holy Roman Emperor Conrad II in 1030, and minor disputes with Poland and Bulgaria, Stephen I's reign was peaceful.

Stephen I then set about converting his people to **Christianity**, using force when necessary. He founded bishoprics and abbeys and made the construction of churches mandatory. He also encouraged his nobles to endow monastic foundations and schools and sent missionaries throughout his realm.

In 1018, Stephen I and the Byzantine emperor, Basil II, defeated the Bulgarian ruler John Vladislav on the battlefield. This victory allowed for the establishment of pilgrimage routes that would pass through Bulgarian lands on the way to Constantinople to the final destination of Jerusalem.

With the help of the clergy, Stephen I broke the power of the tribal chieftains, took over their lands, and appointed counts to administer them. He promoted agriculture and trade and organized a standing army. He also organized a large frontier defense, consisting of swamps and forests, protected by regular frontier guards.

Under Stephen I, the many tribes disappeared as cohesive units, but the fundamental social stratification was not altered. The privileged class was still made up of male descendants of the old conquerors, answerable only to the king or his representative and entitled to appear in general assemblies. Additionally, the landed gentry were allowed to maintain control of the people they had enslaved, although Stephen I freed those enslaved under him. The state only required members of this class to be ready for military service at any time.

Stephen I died in 1038 with no direct male heir. As such, he was succeeded by his nephew Peter Orseolo. Stephen I was later canonized and became the patron saint of Hungary.

The Danish king **CANUTE THE GREAT** united the **English** and **Danish** people and was the first to rule over all of England after the fall of Rome.

Canute was the son of Sweyn I, king of Denmark, and Gunhild, a Polish princess. Though the couple was not legally married, Sweyn I made Canute his heir.

For years the Danes had been raiding the kingdom of England. Sweyn I invaded England again in 1009, and by 1013, with Canute accompanying him, he had subdued all of northern and eastern England. Meanwhile, English King Aethelred II fled to Normandy, and Sweyn I replaced him. Upon Sweyn I's death in 1014, Aethelred II returned to his throne until he died in April 1016 and was succeeded by his son, Edmund II Ironside.

After much warfare between Edmund II and Canute, the two rulers reached an agreement called the **Compact of Olney**. England was divided between them: Canute received Mercia, London, and Northumbria, while Edmund kept Wessex. Edmund II died shortly thereafter, and by 1017, Canute was seated as king of all England. He quickly married Aethelred II's widow, Emma, thus removing any danger that she would turn her support to her surviving sons. Before the marriage, he stipulated that his two sons by his consort Aelfgifu of Denmark would succeed to the English throne before those of Emma.

Canute's first actions were ruthless. He rewarded his Danish followers with English estates, and he brought about the death of Edmund's brother Eadwig. Yet Canute did not rule solely as a foreign conqueror—he listened to both English and Danish advisers. He used English support against external dangers and also to secure his position in Denmark when he went there to take over the throne upon his brother's death

in 1019. It would be some years later, after more than three years of fighting, until he would conquer Norway and become king in 1028. Through warfare, diplomacy, and tact, Canute had gained a widespread empire that covered thousands of miles.

Denmark and Norway were governed by regents Canute had chosen while he was in England. He was an effective ruler in this domain, bringing both internal peace and prosperity to the land. English trade flourished under their king's control of the Baltic trade route. He won the trust of his English subjects by sending the main body of his army home to Denmark and keeping only three thousand bodyguards behind. Probably under the influence of Archbishop Wulfstan, Canute also became a supporter of the church. His law code, which Wulfstan drafted, was mainly based on those of earlier kings.

Canute died from illness in Shaftesbury, England, in 1035.

The man who crossed the English Channel and conquered **Anglo-Saxon** England, was born in Falaise, Normandy (present-day France).

Born around 1028, **WILLIAM THE CONQUEROR** was the illegitimate son of Duke Robert I of Normandy, and Herleva, the daughter of a wealthy tanner. Before going on a pilgrimage, Robert had asked the Norman barons to recognize his son William as the new duke of Normandy if he

should die. When Robert died on the return journey in 1035, the barons honored his wish. But there was much upheaval during William's minority. His two guardians were murdered, and anarchy reigned.

William finally asserted his powers in 1047, when King Henry I of France defeated Normandy's rebellious vassals. William also laid claim to the English throne, based on his assertion that his distant cousin, the childless English King **Edward the Confessor**, had promised him the throne in 1051. However, when Edward died in 1066, the Anglo-Saxon witan, or high council, awarded the throne to Harold II, earl of Wessex, who was more closely related to Edward.

Unwilling to accept this rejection, William gathered an army of Norman knights and crossed the English Channel on September 28, 1066. His seven-thousand-soldier force landed unopposed at Pevensey, England, and began building fortifications at **Hastings**.

Harold II was occupied in the north, fighting an invasion of Danes. With his forces exhausted after defeating the invaders at

the Battle of Stamford Bridge near York, Harold II hurried to meet William. Harold marched his army some two hundred and fifty miles in nine days, gathering inexperienced reinforcements to replenish his weary men as he advanced.

In the lengthy and exhausting battle that followed, William made skillful use of his archers and cavalry against the English infantry. When Harold II was killed, the demoralized English forces fled.

William then led his army all the way to London. The archbishop of Canterbury crowned William **King of England** on Christmas Day in 1066.

Under William's rule, the Anglo-Saxon witan was dissolved and replaced with a royal council, who advised the king on financial, judicial, and military affairs. William allowed the church to retain its lands, but he took over the appointment of bishops and important abbots. In addition, by royal decree, church jurisdiction and lay jurisdiction were separated, and the bishops were given their own courts. This was a decisive step in the evolution of common law as an independent force in England.

Numerous military campaigns, together with an economic slump, prompted William to order an investigation into the actual and potential wealth of the kingdom to maximize tax revenues. The quickness and efficiency of this survey was remarkable for its time, and the result was the two-volume **Domesday Book** of 1086, which survives today.

William died in September 1087.

King of Germany and Italy, and Holy Roman emperor, **FREDERICK BARBAROSSA** restored order in Germany and then spent thirty years trying to restore the glories of the Roman Empire.

When his father Frederick, duke of Swabia (in present-day southwest Germany), abdicated in 1147, Frederick Barbarossa succeeded him. Then when his uncle, the Holy Roman Emperor Conrad III, died in 1152, he was elected king of Germany. A strong, handsome man with golden hair and a red beard, Frederick Barbarossa was energetic, highly intelligent, and a leader of the people.

During his reign, Frederick was kept busy on two fronts: organizing his German feudal estates while keeping the nobility satisfied with concessions, honors, and consultations as well as restoring imperial authority in Italy.

In 1152, Frederick Barbarossa declared a general piece of the land in Germany. It was enforced with the help of ministers, whom he selected from his entourage, instead of the nobility or church as was customary. He was then crowned king of Italy, after capturing and turning over to Pope **Eugenius III** the reforming monk, Arnold of Brescia, in 1154. Eugenius III also crowned him the Holy Roman emperor. After this, Frederick Barbarossa considered himself an heir equal to the likes of Justinian I (see no. 17) and Charlemagne (see no. 19), and he aimed to restore the power and glory of the Roman Empire.

Frederick Barbarossa was concerned with expanding and consolidating royal lands. In 1156, he wed Beatrice, heiress of the county of Burgundy, thereby regaining Burgundian lands through marriage. He then tried to subdue northern Italy by taking the **Lombard** cites, including Milan. Pope Alexander III, attempting to hold Frederick Barbarossa back, excommunicated him in 1160. The ruler did not make peace with the pope until 1176, after the emperor had met defeat in northern Italy at the hands of armies summoned by the pope.

Frederick Barbarossa's many expeditions into Italy weakened his authority at home. Trouble came in the form of Duke Henry the Lion, a Bavarian noble who wielded power in both Bavaria and north Germany. However, by 1179, Frederick Barbarossa was able to confiscate Henry's holdings and send him into exile.

When Pope Clement III convinced Frederick Barbarossa to participate in the **Third Crusade** in 1189, the Holy Roman emperor was joined by **Richard the Lionhearted** of England and **Phillip II Augustus** of France. This campaign was to be Frederick Barbarossa's last—he drowned while trying to cross the swift currents of the Saleph River in Cilicia (present-day Turkey) in 1190. Before his journey, he had secured the crown for his son, Henry VI, whom he also successfully married off to the heiress of the kingdom of Sicily and southern Italy.

SALADIN was a **Muslim** leader who united diverse Arab peoples and fought the combined royal forces of Christianity during the **Third Crusade** near the end of the twelfth century.

Born in Tikrit, Mesopotamia (present-day Iraq), Saladin was the son of a military officer and administrator. At age fourteen, he was sent to Aleppo in northwest Syria to be trained under his uncle Asad al-Dīn Shīrkūh, an adviser to Nūr al-Dīn, the emir, or leader, of the armies of the Muslim caliphate of Baghdad.

In 1164, Saladin accompanied his uncle and the forces of Nūr al-Dīn on a campaign in Egypt, which was ruled by the rival Fāṭimid caliphate. In 1169, after his uncle's death, Saladin became vizier, or a high government official. Under his administration, local revolts were suppressed, Cairo was fortified, and several public works were begun. In 1171, Saladin displaced the Fāṭimid caliphate and was proclaimed the ʿ**Abbāsid** caliph in Egypt.

In 1174, when Nūr al-Dīn died, Saladin stretched his forces and took control of Syria. He gained command of not only Egypt and Syria, but also the Hejaz (in present-day western Saudi Arabia), Yemen, and the coastal portion of Libya. This mean that only the emperor of Byzantium was more powerful. This position allowed Saladin to consider an attack on the Christian-held land that lay between Egypt and Syria: **Palestine**, which the Christians had conquered during the First Crusade of 1095–1099.

During the 1180s, Saladin initiated a holy war against the Christians, mustering a cavalry and infantry of more than twenty thousand. One of the greatest battles came in July 1187 in Palestine at the **Horns of Hattin**. Saladin's forces declared complete victory, and with the surrender of Jerusalem, eighty-eight years of Christian domination came to an end. In victory, Saladin showed a combination of brutality and benevolence. He had all the Christian Knights Templar executed but allowed the Christian population to ransom itself with payments of gold.

However, Christian Europe could not accept this new Muslim takeover of the **Holy Land**. In 1191, forces under the command of monarchs Richard the Lionhearted from England and Philip II Augustus from France arrived to fight Saladin in a Third Crusade.

The Crusaders laid siege to Acre, a seaport city in present-day Israel, and after a lengthy fight, the city surrendered. Philip sailed for France, and Richard pressed on to reclaim Jerusalem. He was unsuccessful, and after numerous battles, a three-year truce was arranged in September 1192. The agreement left Jerusalem in Arab hands but allowed Christian pilgrims the right to visit the city.

Saladin returned to Damascus, where he died in 1193.

- The Catholic Church reached the height of its prestige and power in medieval times under **POPE INNOCENT III**. He instituted the **Fourth Crusade**, convoked the historic **Fourth Lateran Council**, and asserted widespread papal influence over the political affairs of Christian Europe.

Born **Lotario di Segni**, the young man studied theology and canon law, and he rose steadily through church ranks aided by family connections. When Pope Celestine III died in 1198, di Segni was unanimously elected to succeed him as Innocent III.

Innocent III was immediately confronted with the insecurity of papal sovereignty in the papal states. He soon had partial success in regaining papal rights as he brought such states as Spoleto, Ancona, and Romagna under control. But others, such as Florence, Lucca, and Sienna, retained their autonomy.

Building on the work of Pope Gregory VII, Innocent III asserted the right of the Catholic Church to intervene in the political affairs of Christian Europe. The decade-long struggle over the rightful heir to the title of Holy Roman emperor ended with Innocent III appointing his own candidate, Frederick II, as emperor and replacing German influence in Italy with his own. Innocent III used his power of interdiction and excommunication to bring both England and France under his sway. In addition, he fostered canon law, which governed the conduct of clergy, monks, and nuns everywhere, exempting them from certain civil laws and thus reducing a king's power in his realm.

Hoping to unite the Christian Church of the East with that of Rome, Innocent III launched the Fourth Crusade in 1202 to seize **Jerusalem** from the **Muslims**. The Crusaders went against his wishes, though, and sacked Constantinople instead—a move that caused further distracting wars and prevented a concerted attack on Jerusalem.

Innocent III also approved another crusade, this time against the French Albigensian heretics, who denied the sacraments and the authority of the church hierarchy. Force, in the form of an **Inquisition**, along with massacres by papal armies, destroyed the Albigensians.

The Fourth Lateran Council, held in 1215, was the climax of Innocent III's papal rule. Attended by four hundred bishops, eight hundred abbots and priors, and representatives of all the monarchs of Christendom, its decrees were of tremendous significance for the church. Among its accomplishments was a pronouncement that the church was one and universal; an agreement on transubstantiation, which is the belief that bread and wine of the Last Supper changes into the body and blood of Christ; a denial of clerical participation in ordeals such trial by battle; and the institution of more rigorous rules for monastic life.

Amid vast preparations for a new Crusade that he hoped would liberate the Holy Land, Innocent III died suddenly in 1216.

◆ The most feared conqueror in history, **GENGHIS KHAN** united several **Mongolian** clans, formed them into an army, and led them on a campaign of terror and conquest to create the largest empire the world had yet seen.

Born with the name **Temüjin** near the Onon River in present-day Mongolia, he was the son of Yesügei, chief of the Borjigin clan. When he was nine, his father died, and Temujin grew up on his own in a fierce environment of competing Mongol clans.

As a warrior, Temujin set himself apart by combining skillful leadership in diplomacy and battle. Around 1206, the great assembly of Mongols named him "Genghis Khan," meaning supreme leader. Khan then proceeded to unite the Tatar, Kereit, Naiman, and Merkit clans into one fearsome army of Mongol warriors.

The Mongols' swift rise to power came from Khan's dynamic leadership. While the diverse Mongols had long been renowned as warriors, Khan molded the disparate clans into a much greater fighting force that was disciplined, organized, and ruthless. His sons and trusted allies served as his generals, and he was an adaptable ruler who could learn from others.

Khan mounted his first campaign against the **Chin Empire** in northern China. Even the Chinese defenses behind the Great Wall were no match for Khan's forces; they captured the great city of Peking (present-day Beijing) in 1215. From there, Khan turned his attention to the **Khwarazmian** Empire (present-day Afghanistan and Iran), capturing and sacking Samarkand in the center of the empire. Khan sent part of his army north where they entered southern Russia and defeated a large army led by the princes of Kiev. This defeat was the start of Russia being under the "Mongol yoke" for the next three centuries.

By the early 1220s, Khan's **Mongol Hordes**—as his heavily armed horsemen came to be known—had swept across northern China, over Azerbaijan, Georgia, and northern Persia. Khan's forces then conducted a campaign in northern India, destroying Muslim cities there before returning to Mongolia in 1224.

Then they set out again to invade and conquer China, this time attacking the **Xi Xia Empire**, located in north central China. As this campaign was beginning, Khan fell from a horse, suffered internal injuries, and died a short time later. He was buried on a sacred hill in the Hentiyn Mountains in present-day Mongolia.

By the time of his death, Genghis Khan had built the largest contiguous empire in the known world. His successor, his son Ögedei Khan, continued on a path of conquest, and the Mongol Empire would continue to grow until the end of the thirteenth century and the reign of Kublai Khan.

Perhaps the most outstanding figure of his time, **PHILIP AUGUSTUS** of France consolidated the power of the monarchy through his leadership skills. By the end of his reign, his kingdom had emerged as an organized state.

Philip II was born to Louis VII of France and his third wife, Adela of Champagne, making him a member of the seventh generation of **Capetian** rulers. In 1179, when Philip Augustus was only fourteen, his father fell gravely ill, and by the end of the year, the young man ascended the throne.

As king, Philip Augustus inherited a small kingdom, consisting mainly of Paris and the surrounding area, known as the Île-de-France. To increase his holdings, in 1180 Philip Augustus married Elizabeth of Hainaut, an important territory in Flanders. Through her dowry, Philip Augustus gained Artois, a northern French county as well as Amiens and Vermandois.

In 1190, Philip Augustus joined Richard the Lionhearted of England and set out on the Third Crusade. However, before reaching the Holy Land, Philip Augustus aborted and returned to France after quarreling with Richard and contracting the "sweating sickness" that permanently left him with a nervous and erratic temperament.

Philip Augustus was extremely concerned over the health of his young heir, Louis VIII. Philip Augustus's wife, Elizabeth, had died before he went on the Crusade, so in order to secure the Capetian line, he married Danish princess Ingeborg in 1193. A day after the marriage, however, he sought an annulment. In 1196, he married Agnes of Meran, with whom he had two children.

Philip Augustus had a strong desire to increase his land holdings. In 1199, England's Richard the Lionhearted died and was succeeded by his less skilled brother, John. Philip Augustus went on the attack, and after three years of warfare, gained control of the English-held lands of Normandy, Brittany, Anjou, Maine, and Touraine, which he incorporated into his kingdom. During his reign, he quadrupled the territory directly controlled by the French crown.

In 1214, Philip Augustus formed an alliance with Frederick II, the Holy Roman emperor. Together, they defeated both John of England and Otto II of Brunswick (present-day central Germany) at the **Battle of Bouvines** in Flanders. This victory simultaneously added more lands to Philip Augustus's kingdom as well as enhanced his prestige as a leading European monarch.

After this, Philip Augustus turned his energy to domestic affairs. He instituted reforms in law and turned Paris into a major city by paving the streets, building and fortifying the walls of the city, and beginning the construction of the **Louvre Museum**. By the end of Philip Augustus's reign, Paris was rising as an artistic, intellectual, and political capital in Europe.

Upon Philip Augustus's death in 1223, his son, Louis VIII, took up the throne.

JOHN LACKLAND'S reign as king is remembered for both foreign and domestic crises and for a baronial rebellion that led to the first Bill of Rights in English, called the **Magna Carta**.

John was the youngest son of Henry II, king of England, and Eleanor of Aquitaine. John, whom his brothers had nicknamed "**Lackland**" because he had not received lands from his father, was nevertheless his father's favorite. John's brother, Richard I, was favored by his strong-willed and powerful mother. As duke of Aquitaine, Richard revolted against his father's rule twice with the support of his mother: once in 1173–1174 and again in 1188–1189.

For reasons unknown, on the second occasion, John deserted his father and sided with Richard. Henry died before he could mount a fight to defend his crown, and Richard became King Richard I (later called the Lionhearted).

When Richard took the crown in July 1189, he made John the **count of Mortain** (in northwest France), confirmed him as lord of Ireland, and granted him land and revenue in England. In return, John had to promise not to enter England when Richard decided to embark on the Third Crusade.

However, when John learned in January 1193 that Richard, returning from the crusade, had been imprisoned in Germany, he made an unsuccessful attempt to seize control of England. On Richard's return, John hid out in Normandy, but shortly thereafter threw himself on his older brother's mercy and was forgiven. John remained loyal to Richard until his brother's death in 1199, when he assumed the throne.

John's reign was marked with many crises. The first was the major loss of England's territories in France, and Philip II took England's royal and baronial lands in Normandy, Anjou, Maine, and Brittany.

Finances were another concern. King John's inherited estates in England and western France were overburdened with debt. To raise revenues, he imposed ever-increasing tax burdens on his barons and extorted a loan of 66,000 marks from Jews living in England.

The final crisis reflected baronial discontent with John's taxation, war policies, and arbitrary style of government. In 1215, his opponents presented him with a statement of his obligations in the form of a Magna Carta, also called the Great Charter. This document laid the foundation of English liberties and the basis of government by consent of the governed for much of Western civilization.

John's later repudiation of the agreement led to the **First Barons' War**, which ended with the king's death in 1216. He was succeeded by his nine-year-old son, Henry III, who ruled under the guardianship of the Earl of Pembroke.

ROBERT THE BRUCE seized the Scottish throne and went on to lead **Scotland's** fight for independence from England. He stabilized both the Scottish monarchy and the nation.

Born in 1274 at Turnberry Castle in southern Scotland, he was the son of Robert VII de Bruce, the earl of Carrick. In 1286, when Alexander III of Scotland died, both Robert de Bruce and **John de Balliol** submitted their claims for the crown of Scotland to **Edward I** of England. Edward appointed Balliol to the kingship, but by 1296, Edward deposed Balliol because of an alliance he made with France. Edward then declared himself king of Scotland, which would then be governed by English administrators.

The English officials proved to be oppressive and harsh. When a knight named **William Wallace** rose up against the English, young Robert the Bruce joined Wallace's forces, which went on to defeat the English at the **Battle of Stirling Bridge** in 1297. However, Edward prepared for further battle and defeated Wallace's forces at the **Battle of Falkirk** in 1298, sending him into exile and eventual capture and execution. Robert the Bruce, cooperating with the English this time, became joint administrator of Scotland with Sir John Comyn of Badenoch, a nephew of Balliol.

In 1305, Bruce decided Scotland needed its complete freedom from England, and he became the leader in a new war of independence. In 1306, either he or his supporters murdered Sir Comyn, who was his rival for the crown. Bruce was then crowned king of Scotland at Scone on March 27, 1306.

Edward was enraged by Bruce's actions. The English met and defeated Bruce at the Battle of Methven in Perthshire, and Bruce became a fugitive. However, Edward's death in 1307, and the succession of his less effective

son Edward II, aided Bruce. He led a slow and determined effort to capture English fortresses and castles over the next several years. Then, against an English army nearly three times its size, Bruce's forces were victorious at the **Battle of Bannockburn** in June 1314. Edward II was routed and nearly captured, and Bruce carried the war to northern England. Bannockburn was the turning point that confirmed the re-establishment of an independent Scottish monarchy. By 1323, England and Scotland had agreed on a truce, and in 1324, the pope recognized Robert as king of Scotland. While the English made further attempts to invade Scotland, Bruce repulsed them. Finally, they recognized his title and Scotland's independence in the **Treaty of Northampton**, which was signed in March 1328.

Robert the Bruce's reign was brief as he became seriously ill and died in 1329. His son David II succeeded him.

As the first woman medieval ruler in Europe, **MARGARET I** pursued policies that united **Denmark**, **Norway**, and **Sweden**, a tripartite union that lasted for more than one hundred and thirty years.

Margaret was a descendant of Canute the Great (see no. 23) and the daughter of the Danish King Valdemar IV. When she was just six years old, Margaret was betrothed to Haakon VI, king of Norway. Ten-year-old Margaret wed twenty-three-year-old Haakon in Copenhagen in 1363.

Margaret spent her youth under the tutelage of Märta Ulfsdotter, a daughter of Swedish saint Bridget in Haakon's Norwegian court. An accomplished scholar, Margaret's early talent as a ruler soon overshadowed her husband's, and she appears to have exercised the real power. The couple's only child, **Olaf**, was born in 1370.

After her father's death in 1375, Margaret successfully had Olaf elected to the Danish throne and ruled in his name. Following her husband's death in 1380, the Norwegian crown also passed to Olaf, with Margaret again ruling in his name. The Danish-Norwegian union that was to last until 1814 had begun. Then Margaret and Olaf, who came of age in 1385, were poised to make war on Albrecht of Sweden and claim the Swedish throne when Olaf died in 1387. Using her diplomatic skills, Margaret became ruler of both Norway and Denmark, and with no heir, she adopted her six-year-old grandnephew, **Erik of Pomerania**. Joining with Swedish nobles who were resentful of Albrecht granting favors to the Germans, Margaret was eventually proclaimed Sweden's "sovereign lady and rightful ruler." She defeated Albrecht in 1389, though his supporters did not surrender Stockholm until 1398.

Margaret now ruled all three **Scandinavian** states. Her heir, Erik of Pomerania, was proclaimed hereditary king of Norway in 1389 and of Denmark and Sweden in 1396. Margaret retained the actual role of ruler until her death. She aimed to further develop a united Scandinavian state with Denmark as its center, and she consolidated her administration through a network of royal sheriffs. To strengthen herself economically, she levied heavy taxes and reclaimed church estates and land in Denmark and Sweden that had once belonged to the crown.

Margaret also succeeded in foreign affairs. She used diplomatic means to achieve her main goals to end German expansion to the north and to extend and secure Denmark's southern borders. Unfortunately, armed conflict did break out with Holstein in southern Germany. During this war, Margaret died, possibly from the plague, in 1412. Though she left behind a united Scandinavia, she had strengthened Denmark at the expense of Norway and Sweden—a course of action that would eventually cause problems. Her adopted heir, Erik VII, succeeded her.

A member of the family that dominated the powerful Italian city-state of **Florence** for three centuries, **LORENZO THE MAGNIFICENT** was a political leader, politician, and patron of the arts who exerted enormous influence during the height of the **European Renaissance**.

The son of Piero de' Medici and Lucrezia Tornabuoni, Lorenzo de' Medici was a very bright young man, and he was elected to the Council of One Hundred, the main ruling body of Florence, when he was only seventeen years old. Following in the footsteps of his Medici relations, Lorenzo cultivated many political allies and friends. In June 1469, he married Clarice Orsini, of a Roman noble family, further enhancing his power and prestige. When his father Piero died in 1469, Lorenzo became head of the Medici family. He ruled Florence jointly with his brother Giuliano.

The Medici fortunes were in banking and other commercial pursuits. Lorenzo's humanist training, however, left him ill-prepared to supervise all the banking branches inside and outside of Italy. He was forced to rely on managers, but several of them did not serve him well. As new competitors sprang up throughout Europe, he found his power being challenged.

His most formidable rival, the **Pazzi** banking family, formed a conspiracy, with Pope Sixtus IV among others, to overthrow his family. The Pazzis decided to assassinate Lorenzo and his brother Giuliano in the cathedral during Easter Mass. Giuliano was killed, but Lorenzo was only wounded and managed to flee.

When Lorenzo retaliated and the subsequent **Pazzi War** broke out, the pope excommunicated him and issued an interdict on Florence. However, Lorenzo eventually negotiated a settlement and emerged with greatly increased prestige. He then created a Council of Seventy to replace the existing Council of One Hundred, and he put himself in complete control of the new body. Under his leadership, a twelve-year period of peace ensued among the several rival Italian city-states.

A collector of antiques, Lorenzo himself contributed more than anyone to the flowering of Florentine genius during the second half of the fifteenth century. He bought ancient Greek and Latin manuscripts, which he then had copied. Additionally, he encouraged the use of Italian in writings at a time when Latin was the language of literature.

Toward the end of his life, Lorenzo opened a school of sculpture in his garden of San Marco, where he came to recognize a prodigious fifteen-year-old pupil. The young student was **Michelangelo**, and Lorenzo commissioned many of the great artist's early works. Lorenzo's health began to decline about three years before his death. He died at age forty-three, and his eldest son, Piero, succeeded him.

Through inheritance and by marriage, **FERDINAND THE CATHOLIC** brought Spain's two main kingdoms under a joint rule and laid the foundation for the country's status as a world power.

Ferdinand II was born the son and heir to the throne of King John II of **Aragon**. In 1469, he married his cousin, Princess **Isabella I**, the half sister of King Henry IV of **Castille** and the heir to his throne. In 1474, Isabella ascended the Castilian throne, and she and Ferdinand II assumed joint rule. In 1479, Ferdinand the Catholic succeeded his father as king of Aragon, and except for the kingdom of Granada, all of Spain fell under the rule of both monarchs.

From 1475 to 1479, Ferdinand the Catholic had a firm hand in Castile with his young wife to transform the kingdom politically. He revised town charters, making these communities the center of resistance to feudal aggression in the interest of royal order and authority. At the same time, royal confiscations of property did much to increase the crown's finances.

Ferdinand the Catholic also banned all religions other than **Roman Catholicism**. In 1478, the **Spanish Inquisition**—a dark chapter in Spanish history—enforced this ban and bolstered religious and political unity. However, in the process, thousands of people were tortured and killed. In 1492, Ferdinand the Catholic recaptured **Granada** from the Moors, bringing the remaining part of Spain under his rule. The Moors were given the choice of becoming Catholics or being exiled. That same year, Ferdinand the Catholic also expelled from the kingdom almost two hundred thousand Jews who refused to accept Christianity. These measures of expulsion deprived Spain of two groups that had proved valuable as cultural, intellectual, and economic communities.

Spain's era of expansion and imperialism took a giant leap forward in 1492, when Ferdinand the Catholic and Isabella sponsored the first of **Christopher Columbus's** voyages across the Atlantic. This would lead to the establishment of many Spanish colonies in the **New World** and the growth of Spain's international reputation.

Isabella died in 1504, and Ferdinand the Catholic married Germaine de Foix, a niece of the king of France. Ferdinand the Catholic began Spain's struggle with France for control of Italy in the **Italian Wars** and conquered Naples in 1504. In 1512, he annexed most of Navarre, basing his claim on his marriage to Germaine de Foix. After Isabella's death, he retained control over Castile as regent for his daughter Joan.

For the rest of his life, Ferdinand continued his regency over Castile, first in the name of Joan, who became insane, and then for his grandson, Charles V, who later became Holy Roman emperor. When Ferdinand the Catholic died in 1516, he left his grandson a united Spain along with Naples, Sicily, Sardinia, and an overseas empire.

MONTEZUMA was the last emperor of the powerful **Aztec Empire**, which ruled present-day Mexico with a population of eleven million people before the Spanish Conquest.

Born in 1466, Montezuma was the sixth son of Axayácatl, ninth ruler of the Aztecs. Aztec civilization revolved around religion and war, and the young Montezuma was trained as a priest and a warrior. Religious ceremonies included human sacrifices, and this need for victims was the cause for continual warfare. The Aztecs ruled their vast empire more through fear than loyalty.

By 1509, Montezuma had expanded his empire as far as present-day Nicaragua. The capital city of **Tenochtitlán** (present-day Mexico City) was a city of massive buildings, orderly streets, and wide plazas. Its inhabitants had a written language and a very accurate calendar. Tribute in the form of cotton, gold, silver, jade, pottery, captives, and foods of all kinds poured in for the emperor.

The year 1519 brought the beginning of the downfall of the empire. The Spanish conqueror **Hernán Cortés** landed on the Aztec coast with an army of about six hundred soldiers. Aztec priests thought the arrival of this light-skinned man was the return of the legendary god, **Quetzalcóatl**, who according to Aztec mythology, was to return in the year 1519 to reclaim his empire. Montezuma sent ambassadors with gifts to greet Cortés and his men as the Aztec leader hoped the treasures would persuade them to leave. Instead, they made Cortés determined to collect more riches.

Cortés and his army marched to Tenochtitlán and entered the city in November 1519. Though some of Montezuma's advisers thought the strangers may be hostile, he believed Cortés to be their long-awaited god. The Aztec ruler greeted him, and the Spaniards enjoyed great feasts, were given long interviews with the emperor, and were allowed free rein of the city.

A week later, Cortés took Montezuma hostage and forced him to negotiate a truce. The Spaniards occupied the city for months. In June 1520, the Aztecs revolted because they were angry at Montezuma and believed that he had become a puppet of Cortés. Montezuma was killed and Cortés's forces were driven out of the city. His small army might have been completely destroyed if an outbreak of smallpox brought by the Spaniards had not killed many Aztec leaders.

Cortés returned the following year, accompanied by a large army of Aztec-hating warriors from other tribes. The Aztecs put up a valiant fight, but after a ninety-day siege of Tenochtitlán, Cortés razed the great city to the ground, bringing an end to the Aztec Empire. When the city was rebuilt, it emerged as the capital for **New Spain**.

An obsession with producing a male heir caused **HENRY VIII** to break with the Catholic Church, thereby changing the religious and political history of **England**.

Henry VIII was the second son of Henry VII, the first English monarch from the House of Tudor. The young man was educated in the spirit of the Renaissance—he spoke six languages, was a gifted musician, and studied theology and mathematics.

Henry VIII became heir to the throne after the untimely death of his older brother Arthur. In 1509, at the age of seventeen, Henry took up the throne after his father died. That same year, he married the first of his six wives, **Catherine of Aragon**, Arthur's widow.

For the first twenty years of his reign, Henry pursued a life of pleasure, leaving state affairs to his advisers, including his talented minister Cardinal Woolsey. Henry's major concern was producing a male heir, and as Catherine reached middle age without giving birth to one, Henry tried to end their marriage so he could remarry. However, since the Catholic Church did not permit divorce, Pope **Clement** II refused to grant permission. Henry was enraged and took steps to withdraw England from the Church of Rome.

In 1533, the king and his friend Thomas Cranmer, the new archbishop of Canterbury, arranged for Parliament to declare that the divine right of kings superseded the authority of the pope. They then withdrew England from Catholicism and created the **Church of England**, also known as the Anglican Church.

Add to this the **Act of Supremacy** of 1534, which confirmed Henry VIII as supreme head of the Church of England. The Act was the beginning of the **English Reformation**, and created the second major Protestant faith after Lutheranism, founded by Martin Luther in the 1520s. Eventually, Henry VIII began to seize the church's wealth and its land, the sale of which helped sustain his financially troubled government.

In the meantime, the king divorced Catherine in favor of **Anne Boleyn**, who gave birth to a daughter, **Elizabeth I**, but no son. Henry VIII soon grew tired and suspicious of Anne. He accused her of adultery, and she was executed in 1536. He then quickly married **Jane Seymour**, a lady of the court, and she gave birth to a son, Edward VI. Jane died during childbirth, and Edward VI turned out to be a sickly young man.

By the time of his death, Henry VIII had married three more times without producing another male heir. His only son, Edward VI, succeeded him, but ruled for only six years. In the aftermath, there was a bitter struggle between the Catholics and the Protestants for control of England. Ironically, Henry and Anne Boleyn's daughter Elizabeth I came to power in 1558 and reaffirmed England's Protestantism.

◆ The greatest ruler of the **Ottoman Empire**, Europeans called **SÜLEYMAN** "the Magnificent" for the brilliance of his court, but Ottomans knew him as al-Qanuni (the Lawgiver) due to his rigid control of all aspects of daily life.

Born in Trebizond, in present-day Turkey, Süleyman was the son of Selim I, also called "The Grim," who had forced the abdication of his father and murdered his two uncles and more than sixty other relatives. When Selim died in 1520, the twenty-six-year-old Süleyman became sultan of the Ottoman Empire.

Süleyman was determined to advance the **Muslim** cause by waging war on Christian Europe, and at the same time, surpass Holy Roman Emperor Charles V as the greatest ruler of their time. Süleyman began his conquests with the capture of Belgrade from the Hungarians in 1521. The following year, he drove the **Knights of St. John**, a religious order of soldier-monks, from the island of Rhodes. The knights had long used Rhodes to prey on Turkey's trade between Constantinople and Egypt. Süleyman's forces captured Rhodes using conventional weapons of war and bombs—the first time the explosives were used in warfare.

In 1529, Süleyman laid siege to Venice, threatening all of Christendom. Though the defenses of Venice were inadequate and its forces insufficient, Süleyman's army was forced to withdraw due to inclement weather.

During the 1530s, Süleyman's navy, under the command of his grand admiral **Barbarossa**, known locally as Khayr al-Dīn, engaged in warfare in the Mediterranean, while Süleyman marched his army eastward by land. They continued to Baghdad and fought a long series of campaigns against the **Persians** before reaching peace terms in 1555.

Süleyman's final campaign ended in failure. An assault against the Knights of St. John on the island of Malta in 1566 was thwarted by the bravery of the knights and the rocky terrain of the island. The Turks lost twenty thousand men and many ships. Süleyman vowed to avenge the defeat but died later that year.

During Süleyman's lifetime, Constantinople became a center for the arts, with the advent of gem-studded jewelry, porcelain, textiles, and carpets. His architects created magnificent mosques in the great cities of his far-reaching empire. While the population of the empire had doubled to twenty-two million under his rule, rural over-population led to mass migration to the cities, causing unemployment, food shortages, and rising prices. Nevertheless, this great leader brought his nomadic state to the level of a global superpower at the dawn of the modern age.

After Süleyman's death, the Ottoman Empire began a slow decline from which it would never recover. His son, Selim II, known as "The Drunkard," succeeded him.

◆ A ruler who controlled land on three continents, Holy Roman Emperor **CHARLES V** fought a losing battle to keep his empire together under **Roman Catholicism** in the face of emergent Protestantism.

Charles V was born in Ghent, Flanders (present-day Belgium). Upon the death of his father Philip I in 1506, Charles V inherited the Burgundian realm. Following the death of his maternal grandfather Ferdinand II in 1516, he became ruler of the vast Spanish kingdom. Then, when his paternal grandfather Maximilian died in 1519, he gained the Hapsburg lands in central Europe. That same year, after having bribed electors, Charles V was chosen king of Germany. At the age of twenty, he became the most powerful sovereign in Christendom.

The following year brought many changes. In the spring, Charles V summoned the German monk **Martin Luther** before the **Diet of Worms** to defend his ninety-five theses, and Luther's attack on the Catholic Church eventually ignited the Protestant Reformation. When Luther refused to recant his views, Charles V had him banned and declared war on Lutheranism.

That same year, the king began the first of his many wars with **Francis I** of France. By 1525, Charles V's troops soundly defeated those of the French monarch. In a peace agreement the following year, Francis renounced all claims to Milan, Genoa, and Naples, as well as lands in Flanders, Artois, and the duchy of Burgundy. While Charles was increasing his control over European lands, Hernán Cortés was conquering the rich Aztec Empire (present-day Mexico) and accumulating those lands in North America for Spanish control under Charles's rule. In 1533, Spanish conquests would spread to South America with the destruction of the Inca Empire in Peru.

In 1530, Charles was crowned Holy Roman emperor by the pope. For much of the remainder of his reign, he was engaged in a war against the **Ottoman Turks**, as well as a battle to crush the growing Protestant movement in Germany. By the 1550s, Charles had become tired of all the fighting, so he ordered all the Catholic and Protestant German princes to assemble in the city of Augsburg. There in 1555, a settlement was reached that called for the religion of each German state to be decided by its ruler.

While Charles accepted this agreement, he was not pleased with it because it did not provide for the religious unity that he spent years trying to achieve. Weary of the reins of power, he abdicated his claims to the Netherlands, Italy, and all of Spain and its possessions in favor of his son Philip II, and the rule of the Holy Roman Empire to his brother Ferdinand I. Charles retired to a monastery, where he died in 1558.

Champion of the **Roman Catholic Counter-Reformation, PHILIP II** ruled Spain at its peak of power, his empire stretching throughout Europe across the Atlantic Ocean to North and South America.

Philip II was the son of the Holy Roman Emperor Charles V (see no. 38) and Isabella of Portugal. As a young man, he had a privileged education. At the age of sixteen, he married the first of his four wives, his cousin Maria of Portugal, who died during childbirth. His other wives were Mary I of England, Elizabeth of Valois, and Anna of Austria.

Upon abdication of his father in 1556, Philip II became king of Spain. He ruled all his father's dominions except Germany. The title of Holy Roman emperor and the ancient Hapsburg lands went to Philip II's uncle, Ferdinand I.

During his reign, Philip II engaged in many costly wars that tested the strength of his empire. The fourth and last **Hapsburg-Valois War** was decisively concluded when he defeated the French at Saint Quentin in 1557 and at Gravelines the following year. In 1559, the **Treaty of Cateau-Cambrésis** firmly cemented Spanish hegemony in Italy. Philip II also fought the **Muslim Turks**, who threatened Spain's rich possessions in Italy and the Mediterranean. Then, a Spanish fleet achieved a great victory against the Turks at the Battle of Lepanto in 1571.

In 1580, when the last male heir to the Portuguese throne died, Philip laid claim to the crown through what he considered his hereditary rights as his mother Isabella was the daughter of King Manuel I of Portugal. Philip II was supported by the high clergy and part of the nobility, and that, combined with his military forces, helped him secure the crown.

Though Philip II was a conscientious ruler, he was a devout Catholic to the point of fanaticism and was intent in stamping out **Protestantism**. When his second wife, Mary Tudor—the Catholic queen of England—died in 1558, he asked for the hand of her half sister, Elizabeth I, who succeeded to the throne. However, Elizabeth I refused his proposal and returned England to the Protestant Anglican Church founded by her father, Henry VIII (see no. 36).

Unable to forge an alliance with England through marriage, angered by its Protestantism, and jealous of its growing naval power, Philip II launched an ill-fated attack against England in 1588. Spain's massive Armada—132 vessels and more than 3,000 cannons—was defeated by the English as much of its fleet was scattered by a major storm.

Although the defeat damaged his empire and diminished Spanish prestige, Spain was still enjoying immense power when Philip II died in 1598. He was succeeded by his son Philip III.

Under the reign of **ELIZABETH I**, England became an established international power, achieved economic prosperity, and ushered in a cultural awakening during which literature and the arts flourished as never before.

The daughter of King **Henry VIII** (see no. 36) and his second wife, Anne Boleyn, Elizabeth I hardly knew her mother. When she was only three years old, her mother was charged with adultery and beheaded. After the execution, her parents' marriage was invalidated, and Elizabeth I was declared illegitimate. However, in 1544, the Act of Succession restored her in line for the throne after her half brother Edward VI and her half sister Mary I.

By the 1550s, there was bitter conflict between **Catholics** and **Protestants** in England. Elizabeth I's older half sister, Mary I, England's Catholic queen, had Elizabeth I imprisoned in the Tower of London and then exiled because Mary I feared that Protestant leaders might try to place her half sister on the throne. However, when the queen neared death, she reconciled with Elizabeth I and named her as successor.

In 1558, the twenty-five-year-old Elizabeth I became queen, and it soon became apparent that she was more than equal to the job. Using intelligence, wit, and caution, she chose able and wise advisers to help her steer England on a steady and prosperous course. On religious affairs, she reverted England to Protestantism with a moderate approach. She established the Anglican Church's separation from Rome but still based the church's structure on the Catholic model. As long as her subjects attended the Anglican Church, they were not persecuted for their private beliefs.

Throughout her rule, Elizabeth I was determined to avoid alliances with other monarchs through marriage. Despite pressure from Parliament, she refused all proposals and declared herself as the **"Virgin Queen."** Later in her reign, Elizabeth I's rule was threatened by supporters of her Catholic cousin, **Mary Queen of Scots**. Mary had been living in England under house arrest for nineteen years after she was forced to abdicate the Scottish throne. In 1587, when cousin Mary was implicated in yet another Catholic plot against the queen, Elizabeth I signed her death warrant, and she was executed.

Elizabeth I also faced threats from foreign powers—especially Spain—which was fast gaining power throughout Europe and the rest of the world. In 1588, Philip II of Spain sent an "invincible" Armada to invade the island nation, but England's fleet soundly defeated the Spanish forces, which were later nearly destroyed in entirety when a storm scattered the remaining ships.

During her reign, Elizabeth I stabilized England's finances by introducing a new currency. Her rule was also a time of unparalleled literary achievement, when such renowned writers as **William Shakespeare** flourished.

When Elizabeth I's forty-five-year reign ended, the popular and dynamic queen was mourned by the whole nation.

The most famous of all French kings, **LOUIS THE GREAT** led France through an age of political, military, and cultural ascendancy in the Western world.

Born in 1638, the future king was not yet five years old when his father, Louis XIII, died. Until he came of age, Louis XIV's mother, Anne of Austria, ruled as queen regent, but power actually resided with the chief minister, Cardinal Mazarin. In 1660, Louis the Great married Maria Theresa, daughter of Philip IV of Spain. The following year, after the death of Mazarin, twenty-three-year-old Louis the Great announced that he would govern. For the next fifty-four years, the so-called **Sun King**—called as such for the flamboyant brilliance of his court—ruled as an absolute monarch.

The first twenty years of the king's reign were the most successful. The finances of the kingdom were reformed, trade increased, and a strong colonial policy undertaken. The French army became the finest fighting machine in Europe. Theater, music, architecture, painting, sculpture, and the sciences flourished.

In 1682, Louis the Great turned **Versailles**, the enchanting château of his youth located just outside Paris, into the official residence of the court and seat of French government. By providing enough space to house the courtiers, or court attendants, the château and its outbuildings helped domesticate the nobility. Devoting himself to his subjects, Louis the Great put himself on constant public display. The wheels of the administration that he established during the early part of his reign ran smoothly. At the center, the king and council made decisions while, in the provinces, administrators executed the king's orders. The courts were entirely under Louis the Great's control.

During his coronation, Louis the Great had sworn to defend the Catholic faith. To preserve the religious unity of his kingdom, he launched a struggle against the growing Protestant followers of John Calvin, known as **Huguenots**. In 1685, Louis revoked the **Edict of Nantes**, which had decreed religious tolerance. The forced conversions and persecutions that followed led to the emigration of some two hundred thousand Huguenots.

In a series of wars between 1667 and 1697, Louis the Great extended France's eastern border at the expense of the Hapsburgs. However, the last years of his reign brought trouble. In the **War of the Spanish Succession**, the French king engaged a hostile European coalition, which feared French domination in Europe, to secure the Spanish throne for his grandson, Philip of Anjou. While Louis the Great was ultimately successful, the war drained France's finances and effectively checked French expansion in Europe.

By 1715, a series of deaths in the royal family left only the king's five-year old great-grandson as heir to the throne. Despite the brilliance of his reign, Louis the Great left behind a nearly bankrupt and militarily weakened France.

PETER THE GREAT transformed Russia into a modern state, creating a new capital, building a navy, and expanding his nation's borders to gain important access to the Baltic Sea.

Peter was born in Moscow in 1672, the son of Tsar Aleksey Nikolayevich and his second wife, Natalya Naryshkina. The death of his father in 1682 brought about a bloody struggle for the succession between the families of his first and second wives. The result was that Peter and his half brother Ivan were made co-tsars while Peter's half sister Sophia served as regent.

In 1689, Peter managed to remove his sister from her position. Upon Ivan's death in 1696, Peter was officially declared tsar of all Russia.

A huge and imposing figure at six foot, seven inches tall, Peter was both energetic and inquisitive, generous and cruel. From the beginning of his reign, he set out to modernize Russia, which at the time had no navy, no ports, and conducted no trade or exchange with other European countries. In 1697, he embarked on a European tour—sometimes traveling incognito—to acquire the Western techniques necessary to modernize both Russia's armed forces and its industry. After returning home, he Europeanized Russian court life, bullying his nobles into cutting their beards and adopting Western dress. The church became subservient to the state, and the old Russian calendar was changed to the Western Julian calendar.

In the late 1690s, Peter imported ship builders from Austria and Prussia to construct warships and other vessels for a Russian navy. This fleet allowed him to capture the Turkish fortress on the Sea of Azov and build a Russian naval station there. Peter then began a war against Sweden for control of lands on the edge of the Baltic Sea. In the first battle of the Great Northern War from 1700–1721, Russia suffered a crushing defeat at the hands of the Swedes and their brilliant military leader, King Charles XII at the Battle of Narva.

Following this disaster, Peter began extensive reform to modernize the Russian army by hiring architects and engineers to bring in artillery and train his men. In 1704, Peter captured Narva in a siege, and in 1709, he won a decisive victory at the Battle of Poltava. The Treaty of Nystad, concluded in 1721, gave Russia the eastern shore of the Baltic, which was Peter's desired "window to the West."

Peter used some of the conquered Swedish territory to build a new Russian capital along the Neva River, and the city of St. Petersburg would eventually spread to all the surrounding islands serving the river's tributaries.

Peter died in February 1725 after a brief illness and was succeeded by his wife, Catherine.

◆ Brilliant military commander and enlightened monarch, **FREDERICK II** turned his small north German kingdom of Prussia into one of the most powerful states in Europe.

Frederick was the son of Frederick William I, king of Prussia, and Sophia Dorothea of Hanover, daughter of England's King George I. In May 1740, Frederick succeeded his father as king. Later that year, Austria's ruler, Charles VI, died and was succeeded by his daughter, **Maria Theresa**. Frederick used the opportunity to seize Silesia, a rich Austrian province with an advanced economy.

Frederick's actions instigated the **War of the Austrian Succession** from 1740–1748, during which Frederick often played both sides, changing allies and enemies with great skill and duplicity. When the war ended, he still held Silesia—as well as the undying hatred of Maria Theresa and her most formidable ally, Empress Elizabeth of Russia.

Beginning in 1757, France, Sweden, Russia, and many of the smaller German states joined against Frederick in the **Seven Years' War** from 1756–1763. For Frederick, the war soon became a life-and-death struggle. As the forces he could put in the field dwindled and his subjects resisted the unprecedented burdens of the war, the Prussian position became increasingly difficult. By 1761, it was desperate.

In January 1762, the death of the Russian empress Elizabeth changed the situation.

Her successor, her nephew Peter III, who fanatically admired both Prussia and Frederick, signed an armistice in May followed by a Russo-Prussian peace treaty. Maria Theresa's hopes of recovering Silesia ended. The 1763 **Peace of Hubertusburg** treaty left the province in Frederick's hands. Prussia had survived and its military reputation was greater than ever—but not without cost. The army had lost one hundred eighty thousand soldiers, and some provinces were completely devastated. Thereafter, Frederick was determined to avoid another such conflict.

Frederick's wars established his personal reputation as a military genius and won recognition for Prussia. Besides Silesia, Frederick also acquired East Frisia on the North Sea coast. Later, at the First Partition of Poland in 1772, he obtained West Prussia, and thus formed a territorial link between East Prussia and the rest of his domains to the West.

In contrast to his reputation as a ruthless and ambitious military leader, Frederick was also a man of culture and a patron of literature and the arts. He was interested in the new **European Enlightenment** movement sweeping Europe. He invited the great French writer **Voltaire** to Berlin, and even wrote poetry himself. He also made agricultural and industrial improvements and pursued a policy of religious tolerance. Among his other reforms, Frederick revised and modernized the judiciary, and issued a new codification of Prussian law.

Reformer and humanitarian **MARIA THERESA** of Austria was one of the eighteenth century's greatest woman rulers.

Maria was born in Vienna in 1717, the eldest daughter of Emperor **Charles VI**. In 1736, she married Francis Stephen of Lorraine, and the marriage was a love match. The couple had sixteen children, ten of whom survived to adulthood.

Before his death in 1740, Charles VI, with no male heir, altered Hapsburg family law by an edict called the **Pragmatic Sanction** under which Maria Theresa would inherit and rule his vast holdings. Upon his death, she became Queen of Hungary and Bohemia, and archduchess of Austria. However, when she ascended the throne, her subjects were discontented, the army was weak, and her foreign enemies were eager to exploit the situation.

Her claim to the throne was challenged, and she soon became embroiled in the **War of the Austrian Succession** from 1740–1748. By the end of the war, she had lost most of Silesia, a land rich in ore deposits, to Frederick II of Prussia. She was also forced to give up lands in Italy to both Spain and Sardinia. However, with the **Treaty of Aix-la-Chapelle** in 1748, her rights to the throne were acknowledged, and her husband was recognized as emperor.

After the war, the empress turned toward domestic matters and financial reforms. Agriculture, manufacturing, and commerce began to flourish once more, and national revenues increased while taxes were lowered. She appointed ministers to reorganize her armies and skillfully handle foreign affairs.

Even with these successes, Maria Theresa never accepted the loss of Silesia. In 1756, she allied herself with France and Russia against Prussia, resulting in the **Seven Years' War**, which exhausted Europe and left the territorial position essentially the same as before.

When the Seven Years' War ended in 1763 and left the monarchy with a mountain of debts, Maria Theresa became a champion of peace, a reformer and a humanitarian. Her reforms included education, new public health services, codification of laws, and the abolishment of torture. Deeply pious, she nevertheless began to move toward subordinating the church to the authority of the state. Her reign was considered the most moral in Europe.

Her husband's death in 1765 plunged Maria Theresa into prolonged grief, and caused her to turn to her son Joseph, who served as co-regent during the final fifteen years of her life. However, a continuous conflict with Joseph clouded those years. She mistrusted his interest in the Enlightenment and was offended by his admiration of Frederick the Great. Ironically, her own reforms smoothed the road for the enlightened despotism that was to mark Joseph's reign as her successor.

As empress of Russia, the energetic and resourceful **CATHERINE THE GREAT** vastly extended her nation's borders and continued the modernization begun by Peter the Great at the beginning of the eighteenth century.

Born in Stettin, Prussia (present-day Poland), as **Sophia Augusta Frederica**, daughter of a prince of Anhalt-Zerbst, she later adopted the name Catherine upon conversion to the Orthodox faith. As a young girl, she was summoned to Russia by Empress **Elizabeth I** in the hopes of a marriage arrangement to Elizabeth's nephew, Peter, the grandson of Peter the Great and heir to the throne. The young couple married in 1744, but the marriage was not a happy one.

In 1762, Peter ascended the throne. However, his unstable nature and pro-Prussian sentiments made him very unpopular. After a six-month reign, Peter was overthrown in a military revolution led in part by **Grigory Orlov**, Catherine's lover, who was conspiring to put her on the throne. Peter was murdered shortly thereafter, and in September 1762, Catherine's thirty-four-year reign began.

In foreign affairs, Catherine wanted to expand her empire. As a result of two separate wars with Turkey—from 1768–1774 and 1787–1791—she gained control of **Crimea** and access to the Black Sea. She also annexed a vast amount of territory on Russia's western border by taking part with Prussia and Austria in three separate partitions of Poland in 1772, 1793, and 1795.

In domestic affairs, Catherine intended to make Russia a prosperous and powerful state. To replenish the state treasury, she secularized the property of clergy, who owned one-third of the land and serfs. The Russian clergy became powerless state-paid functionaries. Many of her actions favored the nobles, whom she needed for support. She excused them from military service and expanded their rights over their serfs, a situation that led to a massive peasant revolt, which was ultimately crushed by the military, in 1773.

Catherine was influenced by reading the works of the **European Enlightenment** and sought to make Russian society as cultured as that of Paris and Berlin. She corresponded with French writers such as **Voltaire**, brought experts to court to collect art and antiquities, and turned **St. Petersburg** into a cultural center in Europe.

Catherine was a brilliant, forceful ruler who worked tirelessly—she often arose at five o'clock in the morning and worked fifteen hours a day—and she did much to modernize her country. She reorganized the twenty-nine provinces, built hundreds of new towns, renovated old towns, expanded trade, developed communications, and established medical schools and the first schools for girls.

When she died in 1796, Catherine was succeeded by her son, Paul I.

- Leader of the Continental Army in America's fight for independence, **GEORGE WASHINGTON** was the overwhelming choice among the new nation's founders to become the first president of the United States.

Born in Westmoreland County, Virginia, in 1732, to Augustine Washington, a Virginia landowner who died when George was eleven years old. He attended school irregularly until he was fifteen, when he left to become a surveyor. He inherited **Mount Vernon** at the age of twenty and became head of one of Virginia's largest estates.

In 1753, he took an oath as a major in the Virginia militia. At age twenty-two, he commanded the first British forces in the **French and Indian War**, rising to rank of colonel and continuing his command until the end of the war.

In 1758, he was elected to the Virginia House of Burgesses. In 1759, he married **Martha Dandridge Custis**, who brought her own wealth and land holdings to the marriage.

Washington was serving with the Virginia militia at the start of the **American Revolution** in 1775 when the newly formed Continental Congress named him commander-in-chief of the **Continental Army**. Washington's troops won many hard-fought campaigns, including a daring and brilliant attack across the Delaware River that smashed the British forces in Trenton and Princeton. Final victory was achieved with the British surrender at **Yorktown** in 1781, and after two years of negotiations, a peace treaty was signed in 1783.

After the war, Washington was called upon to preside over the Constitutional Convention in 1787, which drew up the Constitution of the United States. Two years later, his countrymen unanimously elected him as the **first president** of the United States.

As president, Washington tried to govern by consensus, relying on his top cabinet appointees, such as Secretary of State **Thomas Jefferson** and Secretary of the Treasury **Alexander Hamilton**. This was often difficult as those two men rarely agreed on policy. Washington was reelected in 1793, and during his eight years in office, Vermont, Kentucky, and Tennessee joined the Union, the Bank of the United States was chartered, and the national mint was established.

Washington could have served another four-year term if he had wanted to, but he refused. In March 1797, he gave his farewell address, in which he urged Americans to avoid the fighting brought on by rival political factions and to remain free of foreign entanglements. His brilliant military and political leadership was crucial to the foundation of the young nation.

LOUIS XVI ruled France during its most tumultuous period, and his inability to deal with the **French Revolution** cost him his crown—and his life.

Louis was born at Versailles outside of Paris. He was the grandson of Louis XV and third son of the Dauphin, the heir to French throne. The deaths of his father and two older brothers made the young prince the Dauphin in 1765. In 1770, he married fifteen-year-old **Marie Antoinette**,

youngest daughter of Archduchess Maria Theresa of Austria.

As Louis XVI ascended to the throne in 1774, France was burdened with debt, and heavy taxation spread misery among the people. Louis XVI immediately remitted some of the most oppressive taxes and instituted financial reforms. His attempts to enact reforms met with general approval. However, his poor judgment left him unsuited to provide the leadership needed to control the complex social and political conflict smoldering in France.

In May 1776, Louis XVI appointed Jacques Necker as director of the treasury, but costly French intervention in the American Revolution undermined his efforts. Necker resigned in 1781, and those who followed him were unable to ward off bankruptcy. He then convoked the Assembly of Notables and requested their consent to tax the privileged classes, but they refused.

Louis XVI finally convoked the **States-General** assembly in 1789, but he opposed doubling the number of deputies from the third, or popular estate. This led to the third estate proclaiming itself a **national assembly**. It renamed itself the Constituent Assembly and drew up a new constitution, declaring that political independence, equal rights, and universal freedom were inviolable rights.

Louis XVI sent troops to Paris, and rumors circulated that the king intended to suppress the assembly. This provoked the storming of the **Bastille** on July 14, 1789, and ignited the French.

At first, Louis XVI seemed inclined to work with the revolutionaries, trying to convince the people that he favored republican principles. However, the queen and Louis XVI's advisers influenced him to disregard all promises and flee to Austria to fight the revolution from there. The royal family fled to Versailles, and in October 1789, a crowd attacked Versailles and forced them to return to Paris.

During the next two years, the king alternately made concessions to the revolutionaries and made plans to escape from them. The queen tried to enlist help from her brother, the emperor of Austria. When the royal family attempted to flee France in disguise, they were apprehended and brought back as political prisoners.

In September 1792, the National Convention declared France a republic. Louis XVI was brought to trial, convicted of treason, and sentenced to the guillotine. He was executed on January 21, 1793. His wife, Marie Antoinette, met the same fate later that year.

◆ One of history's greatest generals, **NAPOLEON I** transformed the French Revolutionary Republic into an empire and conquered much of Europe.

Born on the island of Corsica, he was the son of a lawyer and prominent official. Napoleon I studied at military schools in France, and at age sixteen, he joined the artillery as a second lieutenant and was promoted rapidly.

After suppressing a royalist uprising in Paris in 1795, Napoleon I was given command against the Austrians in Italy. Before he left, he married **Joséphine vicomtesse de Beauharnais**, widow of a noble executed during the Revolution. Their marriage would later end in divorce because she could not provide him with children and an heir.

By 1798, Napoleon I had become a general, and he led an invasion of Egypt to strike at Britain's colonial empire. He also had become immensely popular in France. When he returned in 1799, he overthrew the Directory, the weak government that was running the country. He then established a new constitution calling for a **Consulate** and named himself first consul. By 1804, a vote by the people declared him emperor.

Between 1804 and 1812, Napoleon I forged the largest European empire since Charlemagne (see no. 19). One by one, his enemies fell: the Russians and Austrians at Austerlitz in 1805, the Prussians at Jena in 1806, and the Austrians again at Friedland in 1807.

By 1810, Napoleon I controlled France, Poland, Italy, and every country in between, including Austrian and the German states of the Holy Roman Empire.

In some of the foreign lands he controlled, Napoleon I secured the reins of power for his relatives. He occupied Portugal and placed his brother Joseph on the Spanish throne. In exchange for not being annexed to France, Holland accepted his brother Louis as monarch.

Napoleon I's ambitious attempted conquest of **Russia** in 1812 was the beginning of his downfall. He defeated the Russians at **Borodino**, but they burned Moscow before he could occupy it. When severe winter weather threatened the French supply lines, Napoleon I was forced to retreat. The battered army returned home with only fifty thousand soldiers of six hundred thousand.

This disaster encouraged Prussia and Austria to declare war again in 1813. Despite his brilliant campaign on French soil, the allies invaded Paris and compelled him to abdicate. Napoleon I was banished to the island of Elba, but he escaped in March 1815 and took power again for 100 days. Britain and Prussia then led an alliance against him, and he was defeated at the **Battle of Waterloo** in Belgium in June. He surrendered to the British and abdicated once again.

Napoleon I spent the remainder of his life in exile on the island of **St. Helena** in the South Atlantic Ocean.

Known as "the Liberator," **SIMÓN BOLÍVAR** succeeded in freeing much of South America from the yoke of Spanish colonialism, but he saw his dream of a continent made up of several states united under one banner end in bitterness and sadness.

Simón Bolívar was born in 1783 in Caracas, Venezuela, at the time of the Spanish empire in South America. The son of a wealthy **Creole** family, Bolívar was educated in Madrid, and then traveled Europe, where he witnessed the French Revolution and the rise of Napoleon I. These events made a deep impression on him, and he vowed to try to free his homeland from Spanish rule.

Bolívar returned home and helped lead a revolutionary movement that deposed the viceroy of Caracas in 1810. However, Bolívar was later forced to flee, and established himself in Cartagena, in present-day Colombia. From there, he wrote his famous Cartagena Manifesto, an impassioned plea for a strong central government and a professional military to free his people from Spanish rule.

For the next nine years, Bolívar made several attempts to reconquer Caracas and liberate Venezuela, having alternating luck of meeting success and being driven off by Spanish forces. In July 1819, Bolívar led his forces on a historic crossing of the Andes Mountains, and in August, they won the decisive **Battle of Boyacá**. Installed as dictator of Venezuela, he then set out to liberate New

Granada (present-day Colombia) and Quito (present-day Ecuador). By 1822, he had accomplished both, after which he combined Venezuela with both states and formed the new **Republic of Gran Colombia**, appointing himself as its first president.

Bolívar continued his efforts to drive the Spanish from the entire continent. By 1825, his forces had removed them from Peru, and when he freed upper Peru, it was renamed **Bolivia** in his honor. The following year, he created a Bolivian constitution and named himself president for life.

In 1826, Bolívar tried to form a Great Convention of South American states, but it failed. He was reelected president of Colombia, but opposition was beginning to grow from some people who feared he wanted to create an empire and rule like Napoleon I. In 1828, he was forced to suppress a rebellion that threatened his rule and his life.

In 1830, Venezuela and then Quito withdrew from the Republic of Gran Colombia. Bolívar, now bitter with resentment, resigned as president of the fractured nation and retired to Cartagena.

Simón Bolívar spent his entire life and much of his own considerable inherited wealth fighting for the independence of the South American people. Shortly before his death, he wrote a farewell message complaining of ingratitude and defending himself against charges of personal ambition.

SHAKA was a Zulu chief who established the first **Zulu Empire** in southern Africa and created a fighting force that devastated the entire region.

The illegitimate son of a minor Zulu chieftain and an orphaned princess, Shaka became a top soldier in the **Mthethwa** confederacy, one of the small chiefdoms located in South Africa between the Drakensberg Mountains and the Indian Ocean. A protégé of the Mthethwa chieftain Dingiswayo, Shaka became more powerful than his sponsor. In 1816, he claimed the Zulu chiefdom for himself.

At this time, the Zulus probably numbered fewer than one thousand five hundred. Shaka immediately increased and reorganized the Zulu fighting force, turning it into a formidable military machine geared to total warfare. He forced young men to leave civil society and form a permanent army. He armed them with short stabbing spears and instilled in them a strict military discipline almost unknown in tribal peoples. As his warriors conquered new regions and peoples, Shaka absorbed the conquered men and boys into his own forces, a tactic that greatly increased their numbers. At its height, the army included around forty thousand heads.

By 1820, Shaka had command of most of southeast Africa and present-day Natal. Although he limited his assaults to the coastal area, they indirectly led to the **Mfecane**, meaning "the crushing," that devastated the inland plateau in the early 1820s. Marauding ethnic groups, fleeing the Zulu wrath and searching for land, destroyed the clan structure of the African interior and left two million people dead in their wake.

By the mid-1820s, Shaka had created a single kingdom out of the clans and confederacies between the Tugela and Pongola rivers. He ruled as a despot. His word was law, and his emphasis on military matters created a nation that was maintained by use of force.

In 1827, Shaka's mother died, and he became openly psychotic. In grief, he ordered seven thousand Zulus to be killed. He became increasingly dictatorial and cruel. He practically ordered his clan to die by starvation in reference to his mother. For more than a year, no crops were planted, and the use of milk was banned.

Early in 1828, Shaka sent his army south in a raid that carried the warriors all the way to the borders of the Cape Colony. Instead of allowing the warriors to rest when they returned, he sent them off on another raid far to the north. His actions were too much for his army, and two of his half brothers murdered him in September of that year. Shaka's descendants ruled the Zulus for another fifty years until the British won the Zulu War in 1879, subsequently creating thirteen small states from the Zulu kingdom.

One of Great Britain's most skillful nineteenth-century political leaders, **BENJAMIN DISRAELI** played a key role in government affairs during the height of the British Empire's power and influence.

Son of English author Isaac D'Israeli, Benjamin Disraeli was born in London, of Italian-Jewish descent. His father's decision to convert his entire family to **Christianity** in 1817 was crucial to Disraeli's career as Jews were excluded from Parliament until 1858.

Disraeli enjoyed a private education and was trained as an attorney. However, after falling into debt as a young man, he turned to writing. His first novel, the somewhat biographical *Vivian Grey*, brought him fame in 1826, but his later work was less commercially successful.

During the 1830s, Disraeli decided to enter politics. He joined the **Conservative Party**, locally known as the Tories, and after failing twice, he finally won a seat in the House of Commons in 1837.

Disraeli was an active parliamentarian, but when Conservative Robert Peel became prime minister in 1841, Disraeli did not receive a position in his government—a slight that he never forgot. After a dispute within the party in 1846, Peel was forced to resign, and Disraeli succeeded him as head of the Tories.

During the 1850s, Disraeli twice served as chancellor of the Exchequer—equivalent to U.S. secretary of the treasury—for the **Edward Derby** administration. However, after Disraeli's Parliamentary reform measure failed in 1858, he resigned, and became part of the opposition for several years while the Liberals were in power.

He became chancellor again in 1866 in a third Derby administration, when he succeeded in getting his **Reform Bill** of 1867 passed; it redistributed Parliamentary seats and greatly increased the number of voters. When Derby resigned because of ill health in 1868, Disraeli became prime minister. He resigned, though, after the Liberals won the general election later that year. His bitter enemy, **William E. Gladstone**, then became prime minister.

When the Conservatives came to power again in 1874, Disraeli became prime minister once more. During his tenure, he profited from the friendship of Queen **Victoria**, a political conservative who disliked Gladstone.

Disraeli was most influential in foreign affairs, where he fostered Britain's imperialism. He secured a loan of £4 million to enable Britain to purchase a controlling interest in the **Suez Canal**, a vital waterway linking Europe with India and the Far East. He annexed the Fiji Islands in 1874 and the Transvaal in northeast South Africa in 1877. Early in 1876, Disraeli, arranged for Queen Victoria to be crowned empress of India, solidifying that country's role as the "crown jewel" of the British Empire.

Disraeli's term as prime minister ended when the Conservatives met with defeat in 1880. By this time, his health was poor, and he died in London the following year.

Revered as one of Mexico's greatest political figures, **BENITO JUÁREZ** became the first Mesoamerican Indian president of his country.

Juárez was born in the Mexican state of Oaxaca into a **Zapotec** Indian family. He practiced as a lawyer in his native state and served as state governor from 1847 to 1852. After being imprisoned in 1853 for his opposition to **Santa Anna**, the Mexican dictator at the time, Juárez spent a period of exile in the United States. He then returned to Mexico and became a key figure in the Liberal revolution that overthrew Santa Anna in 1855.

As minister of justice under the new government, Juárez attacked the special privileges of the army and church. He wrote many reforms into a new constitution, which was drawn up in 1857.

These measures separated church and state, ended church ownership of land, and required that cases involving the clergy and the army be tried in the regular courts. However, opposition to the new constitution was strong among Conservatives, and in 1858, the Mexican president resigned and fled the country.

Juárez stepped in as acting president, but soon he and his followers were forced to flee to Veracruz where they set up their own government. The Conservatives then established a rival government in Mexico City, and three years of civil war ensued. In the end, the Liberals won, culminating in Juárez being constitutionally elected president.

Many serious problems faced the new president, including an almost empty treasury. To restore some financial stability, Juárez decided in July 1861 to suspend payment of foreign debts for two years. This action angered England, Spain, and France, and by January 1862, the three countries had troops at Veracruz. However, when Britain and Spain realized that Napoleon III of France was planning to conquer Mexico and control it through a puppet government led by **Archduke Maximilian** of Austria, they withdrew their forces. Napoleon III succeeded in his efforts as the French occupied Mexico City in June 1863. Soon after, Maximilian took control of the government.

Forced to leave Veracruz, Juárez retreated to El Paso del Norte (present-day Ciudad Juárez) at the Mexican-U.S. border. In 1865, the United States, which had refused to recognize Maximilian and supported Juárez, demanded the withdrawal of French troops, citing a violation of the Monroe Doctrine. Under pressure, Napoleon III withdrew his troops in early 1867, allowing Mexican forces to capture and execute Maximilian.

Juárez then restored order, returned to Mexico City, and was reelected president in December 1867. Juárez's last years were marked by controversy and poor health. Still, he ran again for president in 1871 and was reelected, but he died of a heart attack the next year.

◆ Italian patriot and revolutionary leader, **GIUSEPPE GARIBALDI** was the driving force behind the nineteenth century movement to unify Italy for the first time since the days of the Roman Empire.

Born in Nice, in present-day France, Garibaldi came from a family of seafarers. Garibaldi went to sea at the age of fifteen, and by the time he was twenty-five, he was a master of his own ship. Within two years, he also found a cause that would consume him for the rest of his adult life—the fight to liberate and unify Italy.

At the time, Italy consisted of several small principalities and dukedoms controlled mostly by Austria. **Giuseppe Mazzini** had formed the Young Italian Society, with a call to liberate and unify Italy, and it was this movement that Garibaldi joined. An uprising in Genoa in 1834 failed, and though Garibaldi escaped, he was sentenced to death in absentia by the Sardinia Piedmont government.

Garibaldi fled, first to French territory, and then he made his way to South America, where he fought alongside rebels trying to liberate Uruguay. In 1848, Garibaldi returned home as the Italian people rose up again to overthrow their foreign rulers.

In 1849, he led his troops in a heroic struggle in Rome that lasted for weeks against the French, Austrian, and Neapolitan armies. When they could no longer hold on, Garibaldi and his soldiers escaped in a daring march that brought them fame throughout Italy.

Garibaldi once more went into exile. He made his way to the United States and lived quietly for a while in New York. He returned to Europe in 1854 and bought part of Caprera, a desolate island off Sardinia.

In May 1860, Garibaldi sailed from Genoa with one thousand soldiers, his famous **Redshirts**. They landed on the island of Sicily and using guerrilla tactics Garibaldi had learned in South America, they completely routed the twenty-five-thousand-head army of Naples. Throughout the summer, Garibaldi's forces marched across Sicily and then north, crossing the Straits of Messina and onto the mainland, winning one victory after another.

By mid-September, when Garibaldi marched into Naples, he had become the virtual dictator of Sicily and southern Italy. He then magnanimously yielded all his power to King **Victor Emmanuel II** of Sardinia Piedmont, who thereby became king of a united Italy, except for Venice and Rome.

Garibaldi then retired to Caprera as a hero to millions. He fought again in 1866 to take Venice away from Austria, and then served in his nation's parliament from 1874 to 1876. He died on Caprera in 1882 and was mourned by all of Italy.

Leader of his nation during its darkest hours, **ABRAHAM LINCOLN** rose from humble origins to become savior of the Union and one of America's greatest presidents.

Abraham Lincoln was born in a log cabin in the backwoods of Hodgenville, Kentucky. Despite little formal schooling, he taught himself both grammar and mathematics. After his family moved to Illinois, Lincoln tried out a variety of occupations. He then entered politics, was elected to the Illinois state legislature in 1834, and served until 1843.

During this time, he also turned his studies to law and opened a firm. In 1842, he married **Mary Todd**, and four years later, he was elected to the U.S. House of Representatives. He served one term before returning to Illinois to resume his law practice.

The repeal by Congress in 1854 of the Missouri Compromise and the reopening of the debate on the extension of slavery in new U.S. territories drew Lincoln to politics again. He joined the new **Republican Party** in 1856, and two years later, he became their candidate for the U.S. Senate from Illinois, opposing the incumbent Democrat Stephen Douglas. The candidates engaged in a series of debates, and although Lincoln lost the election, he established a national reputation.

In 1860, the Republicans pledged to oppose the extension of slavery and chose Lincoln as their presidential candidate. The Democrats nominated two candidates: John Breckinridge of Kentucky, and Lincoln's senate opponent, Stephen Douglas. With the support of the antislavery Northeast and Midwest solidly behind him, Lincoln won the election convincingly.

In February 1861, a month before Lincoln took office, eleven southern states left the Union and formed the Confederate States of America. Lincoln's attempt to resupply the federal garrison at Fort Sumter in South Carolina precipitated a Confederate attack against the garrison and ignited the **American Civil War**.

During the four-year struggle, Lincoln attacked the vast problems of the war with vigor and skill. By 1862, he was convinced that the Union cause would be even further strengthened by a bold political move. So, he issued the order to emancipate all enslaved people in states engaged in rebellion—a turning point in the nonmilitary side of the conflict. However, the preservation and restoration of the Union were still Lincoln's major war aims, and he expressed this belief in his **Gettysburg Address** in 1863, which is one of the greatest speeches in American history.

Lincoln was reelected in 1864, advocating a reconciliatory policy toward the South after a Union victory. He lived to see the war end on April 9, 1865, but not to implement his plans for Reconstruction. On the night of April 14, 1865, while attending Ford's Theatre, a bitter southern sympathizer named John Wilkes Booth shot him. Lincoln died the next morning, and he was mourned by millions of Americans.

Known as the "Iron Chancellor," **OTTO VON BISMARCK** united the German states, and for nearly twenty years, he was the power behind the throne of a new **German Empire**.

Von Bismarck was born in Schönhausen, Prussia (in present-day Germany), into a noble family whose members had been political leaders and soldiers. He studied law in Göttingen and Berlin, and after holding minor judicial and administrative offices,

he was elected to the Prussian Parliament in 1847. There, von Bismarck opposed the liberal movement, advocated unification of the various German states under the banner of Prussia, and defended the privileges of his elite social class, referred to as "The Junkers."

During the 1850s, von Bismarck was appointed envoy to the Bundestag, or the council of German states, and later served as Prussian ambassador to France. In 1862, Emperor **Wilhelm I** named von Bismarck chancellor of Prussia. Austria was Prussia's main rival for German supremacy, and it became his chief aim to expel the nation from the German Confederation, which the two countries agreed to rule jointly. By 1866, friction escalated into the **Austro-Prussian War**. Prussia was victorious, and von Bismarck formed the North German Confederation, from which he excluded Austria.

The desire of Napoleon III to expand France's eastern border and incorporate many German states led to the **Franco-Prussian War** in 1870. The war ended a year later with the defeat of France. Von Bismarck now easily gathered the German states under the crown of Prussia, with Wilhelm proclaimed kaiser, or ruler. Von Bismarck became the German Empire's first chancellor—a position he held with absolute authority.

To maintain peace for the consolidation of the empire, he advanced a strong military program, gained the friendship of Austria, preserved British neutrality by avoiding naval or colonial rivalry, and isolated France diplomatically to prevent retaliation. With his system of alignments and alliances, von Bismarck became the virtual arbiter of Europe.

Von Bismarck also exerted strong influence upon German domestic affairs. In dealing with the Socialists, he met their opposition at first with extremely repressive measures. When they once again began to increase their presence in Parliament, von Bismarck instituted a program of sweeping social reform to weaken the socialist platform. His reforms included child labor laws; maximum hours legislation; and extensive old-age, illness and unemployment insurance. His economic policies resulted in the rapid growth of German industry and the acquisition of overseas colonies.

The von Bismarck era ended with the accession of Emperor **Wilhelm II** in 1888. Von Bismarck soon fell out of favor and was forced to resign in 1890. He retired to his castle near Hamburg and spent the remainder of his life criticizing the emperor and his ministers and defending his own policies.

The longest reigning monarch of the British Empire, **VICTORIA** ruled England at the height of its power both at home and overseas during an era of profound nationalism and conservative morality that came to be called the **Victorian Age**.

Victoria was born in Kensington Palace, London, and was the only child of Edward, duke of Kent, the younger brother of King William IV. Her mother was the German princess Mary Louisa Victoria of Saxe-Coburg-Gotha. At the age of eighteen, Victoria emerged from a lonely, secluded childhood to take up the throne after her uncle died without a male heir.

In 1840, she married her first cousin Prince Albert, duke of Saxe-Coburg-Gotha. Though it was an arranged marriage, it turned out to be a highly romantic and rewarding one. Albert soon became the dominant figure and influence in her life. He encouraged her to exercise her full rights as a constitutional monarch. Victoria and Albert were married for nineteen years, and the marriages of their nine children eventually linked the British throne to the royalties of Russia, Germany, Greece, Denmark, and Romania.

Victoria's first prime minister, Lord Melbourne, also had a crucial influence on her. He fostered her self-confidence and enthusiasm for her role, but he also encouraged her to ignore or minimize social problems. Under his influence, she became an ardent **conservative**.

Victoria's life changed dramatically when Albert died in 1861. In her grief, she spent three years in total seclusion, and even after that, she continued to wear black and mourn for the rest of her life. During the initial period of mourning, when she avoided any public appearances, her popularity declined.

She regained the people's admiration, however, when she resumed her determined efforts to steer public affairs. She won particular esteem for fully supporting the popular foreign policies of the Conservative Prime Minister **Benjamin Disraeli** (see no. 51), who strengthened the power and influence of the Empire during the 1870s. Disraeli also arranged for her to be crowned Empress of India in 1876.

Conversely, she was continually at odds with **William E. Gladstone**, the Liberal prime minister, whom she intensely disliked, because he favored reforms such as legalizing trade unions and the Irish Home Rule.

During the Crimean War of 1854–1856, the queen instituted the **Victoria Cross** for bravery, and actively supported the pioneering work of nurse **Florence Nightingale**. By the time she celebrated her diamond jubilee in 1897, her popularity had reached its height, both at home and abroad.

Victoria died at the age of eighty-two and was buried beside her beloved Albert near Windsor. She was succeeded by her son, Edward VII.

- Under the forty-nine-year reign of **PEDRO II**, Brazil achieved great economic and social progress and saw its prestige and influence rise throughout South America.

Dom Pedro de Alcântara was born in Rio de Janeiro in 1825. He was the son of Pedro I, the first ruler of an independent Brazil. When he was just five years old, Dom Pedro succeeded to the throne under a regency after his father abdicated. However, the regency was ineffective, and various revolts threatened to divide the huge country into separate states.

To reestablish a direct monarchy, Pedro was declared of age on July 23, 1840. Though he was only fourteen years old then, he was crowned emperor on July 18, 1841. The young ruler quickly used his constitutional powers to regulate the groups fighting for domination.

Pedro II was a calm, serious, and intelligent man, whose reign brought internal peace and economic prosperity to the young nation. Agriculture, commerce, and industry expanded. He diversified the economy by replacing sugar with coffee as the main export, and cotton farmers, tobacco farmers, ranchers, and rubber extractors were rewarded for their efforts. The government encouraged massive railroad construction as well, and nearly seven thousand miles were completed during Pedro II's reign.

After Pedro II had been in power for about a decade, a movement to abolish slavery began to gain strong support. In 1840, Pedro II freed the people he had enslaved under him, but, he knew that due to the power of the landed aristocracy, slavery would have to be phased out gradually. In 1850, he signed the **Queiroz Law**, pledging Brazil's navy to join the international effort to stamp out the Atlantic slave trade. In 1871, the Rio Branco Law, also known as the **Law of Free Birth**, took effect. It stated that children born into slavery after that year were to be freed after a certain number of years in servitude. In 1888, complete emancipation was decreed. Seven hundred thousand formerly enslaved people were freed with no compensation offered to the enslavers.

In foreign affairs, Brazil extended its influence west and southwest throughout the continent. The influence helped overthrow the Argentine dictator Juan Manuel de Rosas, and aided Uruguay and Argentina in a major war against Paraguay.

By 1870, a movement advocating a republican form of government began to spread in Brazil. Pedro II began to lose support within the military and the aristocracy. In the meantime, the emperor's objections to certain laws passed by the Roman Catholic Church strained relations with the clergy.

With these powerful forces allied against him, his downfall seemed inevitable. On November 15, 1889, a military coup forced Pedro II to abdicate. He went into exile in Europe and died in Paris in 1891.

As prime minister of France, **GEORGES CLEMENCEAU** was a driving force in the Allied victory in **World War I**.

Clemenceau was born in Mouilleron-en-Pareds on the west coast of France. As a young man, he went to Paris to study medicine, but his republican politics clashed with the government of Napoleon III. In 1865, he went to the United States, where he worked as a journalist and teacher.

Clemenceau then returned to France to practice medicine. After the government of Napoleon III was ousted in 1870, the Third Republic was declared. In 1876, Clemenceau was elected to the **chamber of deputies**, quickly becoming a leader of the Radical party. A passionate and aggressive critic, Clemenceau soon earned the nickname, **"The Tiger."**

In 1880, he started his newspaper, *La justice*. His reputation as a political critic grew. However, in 1892, he was linked to a scandal involving the Panama Canal, and the following year he lost his bid for reelection.

During the next nine years, he established another daily newspaper, *L'Aurore*. It was through this paper that Clemenceau championed the cause of **Alfred Dreyfus**, a Jewish army captain accused of treason. Clemenceau's staunch support of Dreyfus brought him back into favor with his fellow republicans. Clemenceau was elected to the Senate in 1902 and became premier in 1906. During his tenure, he carried out many social reforms, quelled worker strikes, and took measures to separate church and state. In 1909, he lost the premiership to **Aristide Briand**.

Through his newspapers and public speeches, Clemenceau had long urged preparation for war, which he believed was coming. When the war broke out, he became an outspoken opponent of **Joseph Joffre**, chief of the general staff of the French Army.

By 1917, the war had dragged on for three years, and had cost France millions of lives and millions of dollars in property damage. In November, French President Raymond Poincaré appointed Clemenceau prime minister. Immediately, he began rallying the dispirited French people. He helped persuade the Allies to accept a unified command under the French marshal, General **Ferdinand Foch**. With the addition of U.S. forces, the Allies swept to victory over Germany within a year.

Clemenceau presided over the **Paris Peace Conference** in 1919, and he and U.S. President **Woodrow Wilson** were the major architects of the treaty. However, while Clemenceau managed to restore Alsace-Lorraine to France, the other delegates would not agree with his further demands, which included extremely harsh terms against Germany. The following year, Clemenceau was defeated in an election for president by **Paul Deschanel**. He retired from politics and wrote his memoirs, *The Grandeur* and *Misery of Victory*. Clemenceau died in Paris in 1929.

Under the rule of **MEIJI**, Japan was dramatically transformed from a feudal society to a centralized, modern industrial and military power.

The second son of Emperor Kōmei, Mutsuhito was born in Kyoto in 1852, and was declared crown prince heir to the throne in 1860. His education was considered liberal, though he was trained with discipline and rigor, both athletically and intellectually. After his father died in 1867, Mutsuhito ascended the throne, taking the name Meiji, by which the era is also known. The era truly began with a coup d'état ousting Shogun Tokugawa Yoshinobu and ending the shogunate, the feudal system that had governed Japan for more than six hundred years. Unlike his father, the young emperor agreed with the growing popular consensus on the need for modernizing Japan along Western lines. This idea was a result of the country's recent contact with other nations through trade after a two hundred and fifty-year period of cultural and economic isolation. At his January 1868 coronation, Meiji announced the Gokajō No Goseimon, or Charter Oath, establishing five principles that called for all classes to join together in the governance of their country as well as pursue their individual callings. A year later, he moved the imperial capital from the ancient city of Kyoto to former shogunal capital city of Edo, which was later renamed Tokyo (or "Eastern Capital").

Between 1871 and 1890, the emperor formally ordered the abolition of the feudal

system, the establishment of a new school system, adoption of the cabinet system of government, and a constitution that established a parliament. In addition, he imported machines and tools from Western nations.

As a result of the new constitution, the emperor's political role became largely ceremonial, relegated to the opening of parliament, holding ministerial meetings, and issuing proclamations. Nevertheless, Meiji was not a passive observer of the changes. He made carefully orchestrated public appearances, that, along with his disciplined and frugal lifestyle, endeared him to the people.

The Meiji Restoration's policies were not universally loved, but their effects revolutionized Japan. The unequal treaties that had granted Western powers trade privileges were revised in 1894, and with two victories in war over China in 1894–95 and Russia in 1904–05, Japan showed just how much it had adopted Western military techniques and technology.

Meiji's efforts towards modernization brought railroads, telegraphs and other Western innovations to Japan. But growing social unrest and distrust of wholesale Westernization over time brought about a renewed appreciation of traditional Japanese culture and values, particularly samurai loyalty and social harmony, which were then officially codified into Japanese education. Meiji died in 1912 and was succeeded by his son, Yoshihito.

A scholar turned politician, **WOODROW WILSON** brought high-minded idealism to the presidency, and then was forced to lead his country through the first of the twentieth century's world wars.

Born in Virginia in 1856, Wilson was the son of a Presbyterian minister. After graduating from college, he studied law, government, and history before becoming a professor and a scholar. In 1902, he became president of **Princeton University** in New Jersey, where he instituted many reforms.

He entered politics in 1910, when the **Democratic Party** backed him in a successful bid for governor of New Jersey. Buoyed by his sweeping reform program as governor, he captured the 1912 Democratic presidential nomination. When Theodore Roosevelt's third-party bid split the Republican opposition, Wilson took the presidency with 41 percent of the popular vote.

Wilson brought the progressive agenda he had promoted in New Jersey to Washington. During his first three years in office, he initiated programs that provided federal oversight of banking and Wall Street known later as the **Federal Reserve System**, the graduated income tax, support for labor organizations, and federal aid for education and agriculture.

In foreign affairs, Wilson sought to keep the United States out of Europe's troubles. He viewed the outbreak of war in 1914 as the result of European imperialistic rivalries and sought to protect American neutrality in the face of violations of American rights on the high seas.

Reelected in a close election in 1916, Wilson met with triumph and tragedy during his second term. His efforts to end the war through mediation failed, and in April 1917, he asked Congress to declare war on Germany in response to U-boat attacks on American shipping. The tide of the war turned in favor of the Allies, and Germany sued for peace in 1918. Wilson attended the **Paris Peace Conference** in 1919 and was hailed by enthusiastic crowds in France. While he helped hammer out the **Treaty of Versailles**, he was forced to yield on many points to the leaders of France and Great Britain.

Exhausted and ailing, Wilson returned home to face the biggest fight of his career: obtaining Senate approval of the treaty and America's entry into the **League of Nations**. The strain of fighting Republican isolationist senators proved too much for him. On October 2, 1919, Wilson suffered a massive stroke that left him partially paralyzed on his left side. His wife, Edith, controlled access to him, made decisions by default, and engineered a cover-up of his condition for the rest of his term. Though the Senate rejected the treaty, Wilson never wavered in his dream that the United States should join the League of Nations. He died in his sleep in his Washington home in 1924.

◆ Political leader, reformer, and prime minister, Great Britain's **DAVID LLOYD GEORGE** led his country to victory in **World War I**.

A native of Manchester, Lloyd George was the son of a Welsh elementary school headmaster. His father died when he was one year old, and he was sent to Wales to be raised by his uncle. As a young man, he studied law, and soon became known as a defender of the people against those in authority. In 1888, he married Margaret Owens, and they would eventually have five children.

In 1890, Lloyd George was elected to the **House of Commons** as a Liberal representing a district in Wales. At age twenty-seven, he was the youngest member of the chamber. By the turn of the century, he had gained a reputation for spirited oratory on behalf of Welsh causes. He established himself as Liberal leader and was an outspoken opponent of the Second Boer War from 1899–1902.

In 1908, under Prime Minister Herbert Asquith, Lloyd George became **chancellor of the Exchequer**. He introduced and fought for the passage of bills for old-age pensions in 1908 and national insurance in 1911. In 1914, after the outbreak of World War I, his job was to secure the largest war loans in British history and to stabilize credit to meet the war's demands.

In December 1916, Prime Minister Asquith and his cabinet resigned, having lost the confidence of the country over the handling of the war. Lloyd George then became prime minister and took firm control of the government.

Lloyd George proved a capable, aggressive wartime leader, and the victory achieved in 1918 was won despite conflicts with the commander-in-chief of the British Expeditionary Forces. At the war's end, Lloyd George was instrumental in negotiating the **Treaty of Versailles**, and helped forge compromise among the different parties.

After the 1918 British general election, Lloyd George served as prime minister in a coalition government with Liberals and Conservatives. During the campaign, he had promised comprehensive reforms to deal with education, housing, health, and transportation. The Conservative Party, however, had no desire to introduce these reforms. Lloyd George lost further conservative support when he sponsored the **Home Rule Bill** in 1920 and was largely instrumental in the establishment of an **Irish Free State** in 1921. In October that year, the Conservatives withdrew their support for the government, and Lloyd George resigned. He was reelected to Parliament and remained the leader of the Liberal party.

Throughout the 1920s and 1930s, Lloyd George continued to campaign for progressive causes, although he remained in semi-retirement for a number of years until his death in March 1945.

The most prominent Greek politician and political leader of the early twentieth century, **ELEUTHÉRIOS VENIZÉLOS** led a nationalist movement against the **Ottoman Turks** and spent years trying to turn Greece away from a monarchy and into a republic.

Born on the island of Crete—then a part of the Ottoman Empire—Venizélos spent part of his young life in Athens. His family lived there after Turkey expelled them from Crete because of his father's role in an anti-Turk rebellion. While in Athens, Venizélos became a Greek citizen and later studied law there.

After he returned to Crete, Venizélos became a member of the **National Assembly**, heading the newly formed **Liberal Party**. In 1905, and then again in 1908, as leader of the assembly, Venizélos declared Cretan unison with Greece. However, in both instances, Athens would not officially accept this move.

In January 1910, rebels launched a coup against the Athenian government. Venizélos was invited to Athens, and in October, he became **prime minister** of Greece. He immediately began a program of reform in civil service and education. Venizélos also reorganized the armed forces, and helped rid the Balkan Peninsula of the Ottoman Empire in the Balkan Wars from 1912–1913. In the war's aftermath, Greece doubled its territory and population, acquiring southern Macedonia, southern Epirus, Crete, and some of the Aegean Islands.

At the outbreak of **World War I**, Venizélos wanted Greece to join the Allies but was opposed by Greece's pro-German king, Constantine I. Because of the king's opposition, Venizélos resigned as prime minister in 1915. For two years, the Allies pressured Greece to cease its pro-German activities. In June 1917, the Allies forced Constantine into exile, Venizélos became prime minister again, and Greece entered the war on the Allied side. When hostilities ended, Venizélos participated in the peace conferences in Paris.

In 1920, Venizélos led Greece in an invasion of Turkey. However, the campaign proved to be a disaster. Later that year, the Greek people voted for a coalition of monarchist parties, and King Constantine was recalled. Venizélos abruptly resigned and exiled himself in Paris.

Over the next several years, the Greek government alternated between periods of monarchy and republic. During this time, Venizélos served as prime minister twice in 1924 and from 1928–1932. In the general election of 1928, he won the majority and formed his third and last cabinet. During his tenure, he restored normal relations with all of Greece's Balkan neighbors.

The effects of the Great Depression in the early 1930s weakened Venizélos's domestic position, and he met defeat in the elections of 1932. His political career ended in 1935, prompting him to leave for Paris, where he died the next year.

◆ Known as the father of modern China, **SUN YAT-SEN** founded the Chinese nationalist movement and served as the first provisional president of the **Republic of China**.

Sun Yat-sen was born in Xiangshan, Guwangdong province, the son of a peasant. When he was thirteen years old, he went to Hawaii to attend an English missionary school where he came under Western influences. He later went on to study medicine in Canton and in Hong Kong, where he graduated in 1892.

Committed to westernizing China, Sun turned to politics in 1894. Forsaking his medical practice, he traveled north that year and joined revolutionaries trying to overthrow the Qing dynasty and establish a republic. When the revolt failed, he fled the country, living as an exile from 1895 to 1911.

Sun then traveled to the United States and Great Britain, studying Western political and social theory. He soon began to gain widespread publicity and support for his Chinese nationalist movement. In 1907, he issued his three great principles—nationalism, democracy, and people's livelihood—as a socialism that would provide food, shelter, and clothing for all.

In 1911, Sun returned to China during the revolution that overthrew the Qing dynasty. He was then elected provisional president of the Chinese Republic. At the same time, China had broken into regions that military warlords ruled, and Sun was later forced to resign in favor of **Yuan Shikai**, who had taken over northern China. Sun opposed Yuan's dictatorial methods and organized an unsuccessful revolt. Again he fled—this time to Japan.

When Yuan died in 1916, Sun returned to China, and in 1921, he was elected president of the Southern Chinese Republic. Meanwhile, because he could not obtain aid

from either the West or Japan, he looked to the new government of the **Soviet Union** to help him in his quest to stabilize all of China.

In 1924, he began a policy of active cooperation with the **Chinese Communists** and accepted the help of the Union of Soviet Socialist Republics (USSR) to reorganize the Chinese Nationalist Party—also known as the **Kuomintang**—to hasten the conquest of China. It was transformed into a tightly disciplined body with authority descending from top down, based on the model of the Soviet Communist Party. With a strong party and a strong army, Sun planned to march north and seize the capital.

It was not to be, however, as he died of cancer in Peking in March 1925. After his death, the Communists, led by Mao Zedong, and the Kuomintang, led by Chiang Kai-shek split, with each group claiming to be his true heir. The two groups would wage a protracted war for control of China until the Communists emerged victorious in 1949.

With a tragic combination of cruel fate and misguided policies, the three-hundred-year-old **Russian Romanov** dynasty came crashing down during the reign of **NICHOLAS II**.

Born in 1868, Nicholas was the eldest son of Tsar Alexander III and Princess Dagmar of Denmark. In 1889, Nicholas became very attracted to his distant cousin, Alix of Hesse, a granddaughter of England's Queen Victoria.

The couple were to be married in 1894, but Tsar Alexander died suddenly, and Nicholas succeeded to the throne. The wedding took place one week after the funeral. Prior to the marriage, Alix converted to the Russian Orthodox faith, and changed her name to **Alexandra.** Over the next ten years, the couple had four daughters, and then in 1904, Alexandra gave birth to a son, Alexis. It was soon discovered that the boy was afflicted with hemophilia, a life-threatening blood disease.

As he admitted, Nicholas did not have the temperament for the complex tasks of leading. However, he dreamed of expanding his empire, particularly in Korea where Japan already had a foothold. Instead, Russia's humiliating defeats in the **Russo-Japanese War** from 1904–1905 fomented the growing discontent at home. A revolution broke out in 1905, bringing strikes, terrorism, and peasant violence suppressed by military force.

By 1912, support for the monarchy was wavering. Russia's entry into **World War I** in 1914 made matters worse. With an ill equipped, poorly trained, and badly led army, the action was a disaster.

Nicholas personally assumed command of the army, and in his absence, the empress exerted great influence on the government. She also turned more and more to **Rasputin**, an unsavory self-professed faith healer, who she believed could cure her son of his life-threatening disease. Worthless nominees of Rasputin replaced competent ministers and officials. Treachery ran rampant, until finally, Rasputin's enemies murdered him.

When food riots and worker strikes broke out in the capital on March 8, 1917, troops were sent to restore order. Instead, they refused to fire on their fellow countrypeople, and many joined the revolt. Four days later, the government resigned, and the emperor was called on to abdicate. On March 15, 1917, Nicholas abdicated in favor of his brother Michael, who refused the crown. The royal family was then detained at their palace at Tsarskoye Selo.

In November 1917, **Vladimir Lenin** (see no. 66) and the Bolsheviks seized power. In April 1918, the royal family was taken to **Yekaterinburg** in the Ural Mountains. In the early morning of July 17, a Bolshevik firing squad executed the tsar, his wife, and their children. Their bodies were cast into an abandoned mineshaft and burned. The Romanov dynasty had come to a violent and tragic end.

Remembered as the architect of an appeasement policy toward Nazi Germany that proved to be an utter failure, **NEVILLE CHAMBERLAIN** was the British prime minister at the outbreak of World War II.

The son of Joseph Chamberlain, the well-known mayor of Birmingham, the young Chamberlain was educated at Rugby School. After a successful career in the copper-brass business, he followed his father's path and became active in politics. In 1918, he was elected to parliament as a **Conservative**.

During the 1920s, Chamberlain served as health minister under Prime Minister Stanley Baldwin. In that position, Chamberlain introduced a series of important social reforms in the areas of housing, pensions, and insurance. From 1931 to 1937, Chamberlain served as chancellor of the Exchequer under Baldwin. When Baldwin resigned in 1937, Chamberlain became prime minister in a coalition government formed to deal with Britain's economic troubles.

Chamberlain soon had other problems.

Under Adolf Hitler, Nazi Germany was rearming and making aggressive advances along its southern and eastern borders.

Chamberlain was desperate to avoid a European war, at least until Great Britain could prepare itself better economically and militarily. In a futile attempt to sway fascist Italy away from German influence, he agreed to recognize Italian supremacy in Ethiopia. He also stood aside while Germany occupied and then annexed Austria in 1938.

Then when Hitler demanded that Czechoslovakia (now the Czech Republic and Slovakia) cede to Germany the **Sudentenland**—an area in Czechoslovakia where many Germans lived—Chamberlain met personally with Hitler and signed the **Munich Agreement** in September 1938. In this pact, he and French Premier **Édouard Daladier** granted Hitler almost all his demands in regard to Czechoslovakia. The Munich Agreement became a symbol of appeasement and shook the confidence of Eastern Europeans in the good faith of Western democracies.

When Hitler invaded Czechoslovakia, Chamberlain reversed his appeasement policy and soon proclaimed armed Anglo-French support for Poland, Romania, and Greece in the event of similar attacks. After the German attack on Poland on September 1, 1939, Chamberlain countered with a British declaration of war two days later. He remained prime minister during the initial period of sporadic military action. At this time, Winston Churchill was brought into his cabinet as first lord of the Admiralty.

After Norway fell to the Germans in April 1940, Chamberlain lost the support of many members of the Labor party and Liberal party, and he was forced to resign on May 10, 1940.

Winston Churchill became prime minister in a coalition government of Conservatives and Laborites. Chamberlain served briefly in his cabinet until October 1940, when ill health forced him to resign. He died the following month in Beckfield, near Reading, Hampshire.

VLADIMIR LENIN was the leader of the Bolshevik Revolution in Russia, and the architect, builder, and head of the world's first communist state—the Union of Soviet Socialist Republics.

Vladimir Ilich Ulyanov (he later changed his name to Lenin) was born in Western Russia, the son of a schoolmaster. In 1887, Vladimir's eldest brother was hanged for his role in a plot to assassinate Tsar Alexander III. This unquestionably influenced Lenin's subsequent decision to take the path of revolution.

Lenin studied law at the universities of Kazan and St. Petersburg and graduated in 1891. He immersed himself in the teachings of **Karl Marx**, became a Marxist and began revolutionary activities in St. Petersburg. He was arrested in 1895 and exiled to Siberia. When his exile ended in 1900, he left Russia to continue his revolutionary activities abroad.

In 1902, while in London, Lenin became leader of the **Bolsheviks**, the minority faction of Russia's Social Democratic Workers' Party. While he was abroad, Lenin published many pamphlets and socialist studies, and founded two socialist newspapers. A fiery speaker who was fluent in several languages, Lenin became the face of the movement to overthrow the monarchy in Russia.

In March 1917, Lenin was smuggled back into Russia with the help of Germany, which knew that his position was to remove Russia from **World War I** and sue for peace.

In October, the provisional government that had replaced the tsar was on the verge of collapsing. Using the strength they had established in the "soviets," or unions of workers in St. Petersburg, Moscow, and elsewhere, Lenin and the Bolsheviks seized the reins of power.

The new government's first acts were to propose an armistice with Germany and to abolish private ownership of land for redistribution among the peasants. Banks were nationalized and worker control over factory production was introduced. The Cheka, or political police, ruthlessly suppressed all opposition. The Bolsheviks then became the **Communist Party**.

By late 1918, the Communists were threatened by forces from Western nations and the pro-monarchist White Army looking to restore the tsar. A civil war raged until late 1920, when the Communist Red Army triumphed. In 1922, the Communists brought together all the territories they controlled and organized them into one federation called the USSR.

With communism proving inadequate to get the country on its feet, Lenin introduced the **New Economic Policy (NEP)** in 1921 that allowed some private enterprise. Before he could see it fully implemented, however, Lenin fell seriously ill in the spring of 1922. He suffered a series of strokes over the next two years and died on January 21, 1924.

Undoubtedly one of the greatest public figures of the twentieth century, **WINSTON CHURCHILL** rallied the British people during **World War II,** and as prime minister, led his country from the brink of defeat to victory.

Born in Oxfordshire, England, he was the eldest son of Lord Randolph Churchill and Jennie Jerome, a wealthy American. When he was twenty-one, Churchill joined the army and served in India, Egypt, and South Africa. He entered politics at the turn of the twentieth century and was elected to the House of Commons as a **Conservative**. He remained a member of British Parliament, almost without interruption, for sixty years.

During the 1920s and 1930s, Churchill wrote and was highly public about his support for Edward VIII in the abdication crisis of 1936 and about his vehement opposition to the Indian nationalist movement. He also issued unheeded warnings regarding the looming threat of Nazi Germany.

When World War II broke out in September 1939, Neville Chamberlain appointed him first lord of the admiralty. In May 1940, Chamberlain resigned, and Churchill became both prime minister and defense minister at the head of a coalition government. Using his great oratorical skills, boundless energy, and courageous optimism in the face of the relentless German war machine, Churchill rallied the British people during the grim years from 1940 to 1942 and helped save Europe from total Nazi domination.

Churchill developed a close relationship with U.S. president **Franklin D. Roosevelt** (see no. 71), and in August 1941, the two leaders concluded the **Atlantic Charter**, a statement of democratic principles that dealt with territorial rights and self-government among other things. During the war, the two men were responsible for developing the overall strategy for retaking Europe from German occupation. In 1945, Churchill met with Roosevelt and Soviet leader **Joseph Stalin** at the Yalta Conference to draw up plans for the final defeat of Germany and for its occupation and control after its unconditional surrender.

In July 1945, Churchill lost his bid for reelection after Britain's desire for rapid social reform led to a Labor Party victory. In 1946, on a visit to the United States, Churchill made a controversial speech in Fulton, Missouri, in which he prophetically warned of the expansive tendencies of the Soviet Union and coined the expression **"Iron Curtain."**

Churchill again became prime minister in 1951 and served four years before resigning due to his declining health. In 1953, he was knighted and awarded the Nobel Prize in Literature for his numerous historical writings. While his peacetime government saw a revival in the country's economy, there was little progress toward realizing the united Europe that Churchill favored. He died on January 24, 1965, in London.

As the leader of the Soviet Union for nearly fifty years, **JOSEPH STALIN** industrialized and transformed the country into a world power. However, the Soviet people paid a high price for his official policies and personal paranoia—under his iron fist, millions of innocent people were imprisoned and killed.

He was born Ioseb Dzhugashvili (he later changed his name to Stalin), in Georgia, a Russian colony in the Caucasus. As a young man, Stalin studied for the priesthood, but was expelled from the seminary for his leftist politics. He then became a **Marxist** and joined the Social Democratic Party. After the party split into two factions, the Mensheviks and the **Bolsheviks**, in 1903, Stalin joined the Bolsheviks and became a disciple of their leader, **Vladimir Lenin** (see no. 66).

Stalin played only a modest role in the Bolshevik Revolution of 1917. However, after Lenin died in 1924, he outmaneuvered his main rivals, including **Leon Trotsky**, and gained control of the Communist Party. Over the next few years, he launched a series of five-year plans to collectivize industry and agriculture. Stalin maintained that his program of consolidating "socialism in one country," even though he demanded immense sacrifice and discipline, would render the Soviet Union immune to attacks by outside capitalist nations.

To accomplish these goals, however, Stalin used repressive measures and terror. The kulaks, or farmers who had risen to prosperity, were shot, exiled, or absorbed into the rapidly expanding network of concentration camps called gulags and worked to death. During the 1930s, Stalin orchestrated purges of top Communist Party and Russian army officials to eliminate any threats to his total control. Thousands were shot or sent to gulags, where they either perished or toiled for decades.

Stalin signed a non-aggression pact with Germany in 1939, which was designed to forestall **Adolf Hitler's** desire to conquer both Western and Eastern Europe. Ultimately, Germany violated the pact and invaded the Soviet Union on June 22, 1941. Stalin took over the directions of military operations and joined forces with the Western Allies. The Soviet army fought valiantly on the Eastern front, driving the Nazis back toward Germany. This enabled Stalin to demand many concessions from Great Britain and the United States at both the **Yalta** and **Potsdam** conferences, allowing him to establish Soviet dominance in Eastern Europe after the war.

Due to declining health and paranoia, Stalin only made few public appearances in the late 1940s and early 1950s. His scarcity stimulated public worship bestowed upon him and created a cult following. He increased repression and persecution of his closest collaborators in his later years, reminiscent of the purges of the 1930s.

Stalin died of a cerebral hemorrhage on March 5, 1953.

The first president of the Republic of Turkey, **MUSTAFA KEMAL ATATÜRK** was a soldier, political leader, and reformer who was not above being a ruthless dictator to accomplish his goal of modernizing his nation.

He was born in Salonika, in northern Greece, then a Muslim Ottoman province. In 1902, he graduated from a Turkish military academy in Constantinople (present-day Istanbul), and advanced through the ranks of the Turkish army, seeing action in both the Balkan Wars of 1912–1913 and World War I.

In the aftermath of World War I, Turkey, which had fought on the side of the Central Powers, was divided under British and Greek rule. Violently opposed to this, Kemal resigned from the army and joined activists desiring sovereignty for Turkey. After the sultan outlawed him, he set up a rival government at Ankara in 1921 and became the symbol of Turkish nationalism. His forces drove the Greeks from Anatolia in central Turkey, which left the Greek civilians at the mercy of the Turkish army and vengeful Turkish population.

In 1922, Kemal's government reached a peace agreement with Great Britain. In short order, the Ottoman sultan was deposed, and Turkey was declared a self-governing republic. Kemal was elected president in 1923 and later reelected in 1927, 1931, and 1935 by a unanimous parliamentary vote.

He immediately began a program of sweeping social and political reform, including a vigorous campaign for modernization. Women were raised to legal equality with men. They were also given the right to vote and permitted to sit in the assembly. In Kemal's quest to secularize Turkey, Islam ceased to be the state religion. Civil marriages were made compulsory, men could not wear the Muslim fez headpiece, and women were strongly discouraged from wearing the veil.

Among Kemal's other reforms were the use of the Latin alphabet to replace Arabic script and better educational opportunities. In 1934, he instituted a five-year plan for the development of industry, and the government encouraged agriculture, the opening of mines, and railroad and road construction.

By 1935, surnames, which had already long been used in the West, became a new requirement for all people. Kemal took the name of **Atatürk**, meaning **"Father of the Turks."** When devout Muslims and ethnic minorities such as the Kurds and Armenians opposed his tactics, he retaliated with martial law and the ruthless use of the army.

In foreign affairs, Kemal pursued a policy of conciliation and neutrality. He signed a peace treaty with Greece, a naval agreement with Russia, and settled a frontier dispute with Persia.

While his rule often resembled a dictatorship, at the time of his death in 1938, Kemal had succeeded in bringing Turkey into the twentieth century.

Although his papal reign was brief, **SAINT JOHN XXIII** transformed the **Roman Catholic Church** during the latter half of the twentieth century.

He was born **Angelo Giuseppe Roncalli** to a poor farming family near Bergamo in northern Italy. An intelligent and gifted boy, he was sent to seminary schools to prepare for priesthood before he was ten years old. He was ordained in 1904 and began a steady climb through the church ranks. Roncalli also served as a sergeant in the Italian medical corps during **World War I**. This experience broadened his view of life, and he would be one of the few popes who had witnessed firsthand human suffering on a large scale.

Roncalli became a monsignor in 1921 and was raised to archbishop in 1925. He was then sent on many prestigious diplomatic assignments. He spent nearly twenty years in the eastern Mediterranean, and during World War II, he played an important role in rescuing Jews in Hungary, Bulgaria, and Turkey.

In 1944, he was appointed papal nuncio—the highest-ranking papal representative—to the newly liberated Paris, and he used his diplomatic skills to reconcile clergy and Catholic citizens who had resisted the Nazis with those who had collaborated. In 1953, he became a cardinal and served as patriarch of Venice.

Pope Pius XII died in 1958, and although the seventy-seven-year-old Roncalli had achieved great stature within the church, there was still great surprise when he was elected pope.

John XXIII surprised many people by summoning a **Vatican Council**, a meeting of three thousand of the world's Catholic bishops, as well as lay Catholics. The Council's task was to bring the church, which had lost touch with the political, scientific, and technological changes of the past 100 years, up to date and reinvigorate its reputation. In October 1962, John XXIII presided over the Council's first session personally. As a great reconciler, he cordially received Eastern Orthodox, Anglican, and Protestant religious leaders, inviting them to send observers to the Council.

John XXIII also embarked upon a new start toward Christian unity—to lay aside past hostilities and acknowledge Catholics' share of the responsibility for a divided Christianity.

He sent representatives to the 1961 **World Council of Churches** in New Delhi, India, whereas earlier popes had spurned this organization. He also named the first Indian and African cardinals.

John XXIII's greatest claim to world affection, however, rested on his warm personality. He was extremely open and mingled freely with his flock, visiting prisons and schools and meeting with diverse groups, many of whom were non-Catholics. At the time of his death in 1963, he was one the best-loved men in the world, admired by Catholics and non-Catholics alike.

◆ The most influential U.S. president of the twentieth century, **FRANKLIN D. ROOSEVELT** served as his nation's leader during one of the most turbulent periods of American history—the **Great Depression** and **World War II.**

Franklin Delano Roosevelt was born into a wealthy Anglo-Dutch American family in Hyde Park, New York. In 1905, he married his distant cousin, **Eleanor Roosevelt**. He entered politics in 1911 when he was elected New York state senator. He then went on to become assistant secretary of the navy from 1913–1920 and ran unsuccessfully as the **Democratic** candidate for vice president in 1920. The following year, though, tragedy struck—he contracted polio, a crippling disease that left him paralyzed from the waist down. However, he overcame his handicap, and in 1928, he was elected governor of New York and was reelected in 1930.

Then, in 1932, a desperate nation deeply mired in the Great Depression overwhelmingly elected Roosevelt president. Over the next four years, he introduced several new programs to try to restore the U.S. economy. He spoke often to the nation in his "fireside chats," and his confident, optimistic demeanor in the face of America's darkest economic period helped give the people hope. Many of the administration's programs eased the crisis, and in 1936, Roosevelt was overwhelmingly reelected to a second term.

Soon after World War II broke out in 1939, Roosevelt—fearful that America would eventually be drawn into the conflict—launched a vast rearmament program and instituted policies that would supply armaments to the European Allies.

In the summer of 1940, after France fell and while the Germans were bombing Great Britain, Roosevelt increased aid to the Allies. With war looming closer to home, Roosevelt broke a long-standing precedent in running for a third term. The country had such confidence in his leadership that, once again, he was easily reelected.

On December 7, 1941, the Japanese attack on **Pearl Harbor** plunged the United States into war. Now Roosevelt took the lead in establishing a grand alliance among all the countries fighting the Axis powers. Along with Winston Churchill and Joseph Stalin, Roosevelt developed the overall strategy that the Allies used to win the war.

In 1944, with the inevitable Allied victory in sight, Roosevelt ran for a fourth term as president, and won easily. In early 1945, Roosevelt met Churchill and Stalin at the Yalta Conference to plan the political framework for the postwar world. On April 12, 1945, about a month before Germany surrendered to the Allies, Roosevelt died suddenly from a cerebral hemorrhage at the so-called Little White House in Warm Springs, Georgia. Millions of people, both home and abroad, mourned his death.

BENITO MUSSOLINI came to power in Italy during the 1920s, promising to restore the glory of the Roman Empire. Instead, he led his country into a disastrous alliance with **Nazi Germany** that brought about its destruction and humiliating defeat in **World War II**.

Mussolini was born in 1883 in Predappio in northern Italy, the son of a blacksmith. In 1902, he immigrated to Switzerland, where he was imprisoned more than once for inciting violence during trade union strikes. After returning to Italy, Mussolini became active in the Socialist Party, but he was expelled in 1914 because he favored Italy's entrance in World War I.

In 1919, he formed a new political party. It was a fascist movement that was anti-socialist, anti-communist, but also anti-capitalist. Called the **Blackshirts** because of their military style outfits, Mussolini's group promised to solve Italy's economic problems with a strong central government based in Rome.

In October 1922, Mussolini led a massive **March on Rome**, backed by thousands of supporters. Faced with Mussolini's growing strength and popularity, the king appointed him prime minister.

Mussolini quickly moved to take full control of the government. The parliamentary system was virtually abolished, law codes were rewritten, and he personally chose newspaper editors. Those who resisted him were treated ruthlessly. He won the cooperation of his financial backers by transferring a number of industries from public to private ownership. At the same time, he improved conditions for working people and created many public works projects.

By the 1930s, Mussolini began to concentrate on foreign policy, trying to restore Italy to the days of the Roman Empire through conquest. His forces conquered **Albania** and **Ethiopia**, and beginning in 1936, Mussolini formed close ties with Germany and its Nazi leader, **Adolf Hitler**.

Mussolini's armed forces were completely unprepared when Hitler's invasion of Poland in 1939 led to the outbreak of World War II. Mussolini decided to remain "non-belligerent" until he felt certain which side would win. Only after the fall of France in June 1940 did he declare war on the Allies. In 1941, he followed Hitler in declaring war on the United States.

Following Italian defeats on all fronts and the Anglo-American landing in Sicily in 1943, most of Mussolini's colleagues turned against him, and he was arrested. Rescued by the Germans several months later, he set up a Republican Fascist state in northern Italy, but he was little more than a puppet of the German army. Increasingly, he tried to shift the blame for defeat onto the Italian people.

In April 1945, just before the Allied armies reached Milan, Mussolini, along with his mistress Clara Petacci, were caught by Italian partisans and executed.

A Zionist political leader, **DAVID BEN-GURION** became the first prime minister of the newly formed nation of **Israel**.

Born in Płońsk, Poland, Ben-Gurion received a traditional Jewish education. As a young man, he became interested in **Zionism**, or the late nineteenth-century worldwide movement for the establishment of an official Jewish state in **Palestine**. Between 1904 and 1906, he worked as a teacher in Warsaw and was involved in Labor Zionist politics. In 1906, he immigrated to Palestine, which was, at the time, part of the Ottoman Empire. During World War I, Ben-Gurion fought with the English against the Turks. After the war, he returned to Palestine, which was now under English rule, and became active in the Zionist movement.

In 1921, Ben-Gurion became secretary-general of the Jewish Labor Federation. In 1930, he was elected leader of the **Mapai Party**, the socialist faction within the World Zionist Organization.

Ben-Gurion helped lead the struggle for the creation of a Jewish state. His program of **Zionist Socialism** described the economic, industrial, agricultural, educational, military, and cultural infrastructure on which the future Jewish state would be built.

While calling for a strong Jewish defense force, Ben-Gurion also realized the need to maintain working relations with the British government as long as the Jewish community in Palestine was small and relatively weak. The situation worsened in May 1939 when the British limited Jewish immigration to Palestine and all but banned the sale of land to Jews there.

In 1945, Ben-Gurion visited the **Holocaust** survivors in camps in Germany and became convinced that the immediate establishment of a Jewish state was imperative. He pushed for an anti-British policy of resistance and began to muster an underground army, the Haganah, for the impending struggle for independence.

In 1947, the British turned the entire Palestine question over to the United Nations, and in 1948, the UN voted to partition Palestine into one Arab state and one Jewish state. Ben-Gurion then proclaimed the birth of the nation of Israel in May 1948.

Ben-Gurion became Israel's first prime minister and minister for defense, serving in those positions until 1953, and then after a two-year absence, he served again from 1958–1963. During this critical period, Israel fought and won several small wars against its Arab neighbors, received and absorbed over a million immigrants, developed the economy, and forged its diplomatic position in the world.

Ben-Gurion retired in 1963 but came back to politics two years later to lead a new coalition of Labor Party members who favored a more "hawkish" strategy in dealing with Israel's Arab enemies. In 1970, Ben-Gurion retired for good from all political activity. He died in 1973.

Soldier and political leader **CHIANG KAI-SHEK** led the Nationalist government in China from 1928 to 1949, at which point he lost a civil war to the Chinese Communists.

Born in Fenghua, Zhejiang province, Chiang was the son of a salt merchant. As a young man, he was educated in military schools in China and Japan. In 1911, he joined the forces of revolution and reform inside China, but in the aftermath of the revolution, Chiang supported the republican government of Dr. **Sun Yat-sen** (see no. 63), leader of the Nationalist Party.

In 1921, when Sun was elected president of the Southern Chinese Republic, Chiang served as his military aide. In 1923, Sun sent Chiang to the Soviet Union to study military organization and to seek aid for his regime. When Chiang returned, he was appointed commandant of the newly established **Whampoa Military Academy** near Canton. Soviet advisers poured into Canton, and Chinese Communists were admitted into the Nationalist party.

Chiang's prominence in the party grew after Sun Yat-sen's death in 1925. However, the Chinese Communists quickly gained strength, and tensions developed between them and the more conservative elements among the Nationalists, led by Chiang. With the Whampoa army behind him, Chiang met this threat with consummate shrewdness as he attempted to stem the growing communist influence without losing Soviet support.

In 1927, he began a long civil war against the Communists, led by **Mao Zedong** (see no. 79), and he lost the support of the Soviets. The next year, Chiang became head of the Nationalist government in Nanjing and leader of all Chinese Nationalist forces.

The Communists, the Chinese warlords, and the Japanese all remained a threat to Chiang's government. When war broke out with Japan in 1937, Chiang was compelled to form an alliance with the Communists to fight the Japanese invaders. During World War II, Chiang met with U.S. President **Franklin D. Roosevelt** and Britain's Prime Minister **Winston Churchill**. When the war ended, the Allies recognized Chiang as China's legitimate ruler, but internally, Chiang's government showed signs of decay. By 1949, he had lost mainland China to Mao's Communists, who established the People's Republic of China.

By 1950, Chiang and the Nationalist government had been driven from the mainland to the island of **Taiwan** (Formosa) where he became a virtual dictator. He reorganized his military forces and then instituted limited democratic reforms. Over the years, Taiwan's economy grew strong, thanks to much support from the United States.

Chiang's international position was weakened considerably in 1971 when the United Nations expelled his regime and accepted the Communists as the sole legitimate government of China. He remained president of Taiwan until his death in 1975.

Regarded as history's most evil dictator, **ADOLF HITLER** used his power to build a German war machine that devastated Europe for six years, while he instituted genocidal policies and murdered more than six million Jews.

Adolf Hitler was born in Braunau, Austria. He joined the German Army in World War I, in which he was wounded and awarded the Iron Cross for bravery. In 1919, he helped form the **National Socialist German Workers' Party**, or Nazi Party for short, becoming chair by 1921.

In 1923, Hitler and his supporters attempted to overthrow the Bavarian government during the **Munich** (Beer Hall) **Putsch**. He was arrested and imprisoned, and while in jail, he wrote his political testament, *Mein Kampf* (*My Struggle*), a work full of hateful ideology toward the Jews and ideas of German world domination.

In 1929, Hitler took advantage of the country's economic depression and offered distraught Germans a scapegoat and a solution to their crisis. He promised security to workers, control of trade unions, and revenge against the "Jew financiers" that he blamed for Germany's defeat in World War I.

By 1932, the Nazis had gained widespread support. Although Hitler ran unsuccessfully against **Paul von Hindenburg** for president in 1932, the aging leader later appointed Hitler chancellor in an effort to control him. When Hindenburg died in 1934,

Hitler combined the presidency and chancellorship and became **Der Führer**, or leader. He suspended the constitution, used secret police called the Gestapo to silence all opposition, and turned Germany into a fascist state.

In 1938, Hitler annexed both Austria and the Czech Sudetenland to Germany. On September 1, 1939, he ordered the invasion of Poland, causing the outbreak of **World War II**. The German army rolled across Europe in the early years of the war, but only the resistance of Great Britain and Russia prevented Hitler from conquering the entire continent. By late 1943, the war had turned in favor of the Allies with large-scale American assistance, while Hitler led Germany down a path of unprecedented destruction.

Throughout the war, Hitler was also determined to rid the continent of Jews. He ordered all Jews to be deported to concentration camps in Germany and Poland, where many of them were either worked to death or perished from the inhumane conditions. Beginning in the early 1940s, Hitler instituted the "final solution," or the killings of Jews in gas chambers. By the time the Allies liberated the camps, six million Jews—along with various other "undesirables" such as gypsies and LGBTQIA+ citizens—had already been murdered.

In April 1945, with the Allied armies closing in, Hitler retreated to a bunker in Berlin where he killed his partner Eva Braun and committed suicide. His aides then burned their bodies.

CHARLES DE GAULLE led France's resistance to the Nazis during **World War II** and went on to become his nation's president.

Born in Lille, the son of a teacher, de Gaulle was educated at the Saint-Cyr military academy, where he graduated in 1912. He served in World War I, where he was wounded three times and captured as a prisoner of war. After the war, de Gaulle became a college lecturer and wrote several books and articles on military subjects.

When World War II broke out, de Gaulle commanded a tank brigade attached to the Fifth Army. In May of 1940, he was made interim brigadier general, retaining this rank for the rest of his life. When France fell to the Germans in June, de Gaulle strongly opposed the armistice that established the **Vichy** government. He escaped to England, where he became the leader of the French resistance.

In 1943, de Gaulle moved to Algiers, a French territory, and became head of the **French Committee of National Liberation**, a group that was formed to coordinate efforts to free France from Nazi control. The Allies gave him the privilege of leading French troops into Paris in August 1944 when it was liberated.

In 1945, he was elected president of the provisional government. He resigned after ten weeks, following disagreement over the constitution adopted by the Fourth French Republic. By the early 1950s, he had withdrawn from politics and resumed a **writing** career.

He reentered politics in 1958, when a new constitution was put in place that embodied de Gaulle's conceptions of how France should be governed. Executive power increased considerably at the expense of the National Assembly. De Gaulle was elected president in December 1958, and under the new **Fifth Republic**, he appointed a new government.

The most immediate problems facing the new president were the Algerian conflict and an economic crisis at home. De Gaulle pushed through economic recovery measures, and in March 1962, an agreement was reached granting Algeria full independence.

De Gaulle was reelected president in 1965 and began to push France toward an independent foreign policy. To this end, in 1966, he withdrew France from the **North American Treaty Organization (NATO)** and embarked on a policy of nuclear deterrent. He also signed a historic reconciliation treaty with West Germany, and blocked Britain's entry into the European Economic Community.

Though de Gaulle won an overwhelming victory in the 1968 election, his presidency was severely shaken by the "student revolution" and worker protests that swept France that year. He resigned the following year after his proposed constitutional changes were rejected by the voters.

De Gaulle then retired and resumed the writing of his memoirs. He died in 1970.

The last emperor of Ethiopia, **HAILE SELASSIE** sought to modernize his country and make it a leader in post World War II **Africa**.

He was born Tafari Makonnen, near Harer, and was a grandnephew of Emperor Menilek II. In 1911, Makonnen married Wayzaro Menen, Menilek's great granddaughter. The emperor recognized Makonnen's intellectual abilities and promoted him to government office, where he followed progressive policies and developed a salaried civil service career. When Menilek's daughter became empress in 1917, Makonnen became regent and heir to the throne.

During the 1920s, he began to essentially control the government. By establishing provincial schools, strengthening the police forces, and outlawing feudal taxation, he sought to both help his people and increase the authority of the central government. In an effort to establish his nation as a modern state, he succeeded in gaining Ethiopia's admission into the **League of Nations** in 1923. He was crowned king in 1928, and upon the death of the empress in 1930, he became emperor, taking the name Haile Selassie I, also known as "Might of the Trinity."

In 1931, Selassie I granted his subjects a constitution. Although limited, it established a parliament and a court system. When Italy invaded Ethiopia in 1935, Selassie I offered resistance and made an impressive but vain plea for help from the League of Nations. He lost power and went into exile in England.

With British assistance, he regained power and returned to Ethiopia in 1942.

After he was reinstated as emperor, Selassie I received massive aid from Britain, the United States, and later the United Nations. He implemented programs of economic and educational reform to help modernize the country. Among his accomplishments were major land reform, emancipation of enslaved people, and a revised and somewhat broadened constitution that guaranteed universal suffrage.

Beginning in the 1950s, Selassie I also became the focus of a **Rastafarian religious** cult, which regarded him as a divine being who would lead the world's Black population back to an earthly paradise in Africa.

In 1963, Selassie I helped found the **Organization of African Unity** (OAU), with its headquarters in Addis Ababa. The OAU promoted the unity and solidarity of African states and the elimination of all forms of colonialism. While the OAU increased his prestige, by 1974, famine, worsening unemployment, and the political stagnation of his government led the army to depose Selassie I.

The army established a provisional military government that espoused Marxist ideologies. The monarchy was abolished, and Selassie I was kept under house arrest in the palace for the rest of his life. He died in 1975 under unexplained circumstances. Evidence later emerged suggesting that he had been killed on the orders of the military government.

General **FRANCISCO FRANCO** led the Nationalist forces that overthrew the Second Spanish Republic during the **Spanish Civil War** and became dictator of a right-wing government that he controlled until his death.

Franco was born in El Ferrol, Spain, the son of an officer in the Spanish Naval Administrative Corps. At a young age, he graduated from the military academy at Toledo in 1910 and entered the army.

From 1912–1927, Franco commanded troops in Spanish Morocco, helping to suppress a rebellion against colonial domination. At the age of thirty-two, he was promoted to the rank of general, becoming the youngest in his nation at that level.

After the Spanish king abdicated in 1931, the leaders of the new Spanish Republic adopted a sharply anti-military policy, and Franco's career was temporarily halted until conservative forces gained control in 1933 and restored Franco to active command. In 1935, he was appointed chief of the Spanish army's general staff.

After leftists won national elections in 1935, Franco helped lead a military revolt to overthrow the Republican government. Civil War broke out in 1936, and Franco became commander-in-chief of the Nationalist forces. In 1937, he forged the anti-Republican movement under the fascist **Falange Party**, which he headed. With major assistance from Europe's two other fascist leaders—Italy's **Mussolini** and Germany's Hitler—Franco's army eventually defeated the Republican forces.

In 1939, Franco proclaimed himself leader and took full control of the government. He dealt ruthlessly with his opposition and established a firmly controlled corporate state. Despite pressure from the Axis powers, and his obvious sympathy toward their cause, Franco kept Spain a nonbelligerent nation in World War II. This was one reason his government survived after the Allies defeated Italy and Germany.

In 1947, he reorganized the government, passing a law of succession that declared Spain a monarchy, naming himself head of state for life. Franco established diplomatic relations with the United States and other members of the United Nations in 1950. During the height of the Cold War, he secured massive U.S. economic aid in return for allowing U.S. military bases to be built in Spain.

From 1959 onward, Franco increasingly depended on the **Roman Catholic Church** to maintain a patriarchal society and control over the population in the countryside. The country's hard times forced him to reluctantly pursue a more liberal economic policy. While the regime was forced to grant some social and political liberties, it remained extreme with regard to the Basque provinces, where the government waged a fierce struggle against separatists.

Shortly before Franco's death in November 1975, he named Prince Juan Carlos to rule as king and successor.

◆ **MAO ZEDONG** led the **communist** takeover of the world's most populous nation and founded the **People's Republic of China**.

Mao was born into a peasant family in Hunan province in 1893. In 1911, he fought in the Chinese Revolution that overthrew the **Qing** dynasty and resulted in China becoming a republic. By 1919 Mao had converted to **Marxism** and helped found the Chinese Communist Party. He

also became a political organizer for the Kuomintang, the National People's party formed by Dr. Sun Yat-sen (see no. 63).

When Sun Yat-sen died in 1925, **Chiang Kai-shek** (see no. 74) became the leader of the Kuomintang. Strongly anti-communist, Chiang expelled most socialists from the Kuomintang, and in 1926, carried out a military coup against the Communists. Mao and his supporters fled to the countryside.

By 1934, Chiang's Nationalist forces had the much smaller Communist Army on the run. Mao then led his followers on a six-thousand-mile-long **Long March**. Perhaps only four thousand out of some eighty-six thousand survived the grueling journey to the northern mountains, but the march brought Mao and his supporters international fame, and they gained many new recruits.

After the Japanese invasion of China in 1937, the Communists and Nationalists forged an uneasy alliance to fight a common enemy. After the Japanese were evicted in 1945, they resumed their conflict. While Chiang's forces held many of the cities,

Mao had overwhelming strength among the peasants in the countryside, and by 1949 the Communists had driven the Nationalists from the mainland. Chiang Kai-shek and his followers retreated to Taiwan, and on October 1, 1949, Mao proclaimed the new communist state, the People's Republic of China.

In 1950, Mao signed a treaty with the **Soviet Union**, and benefited from Soviet economic aid. Domestically, his **Great Leap Forward** in 1958, a plan for economic and political development, turned the peasants' lives upside down as enormous new social units replaced their collective farms. The results were disastrous and as many as twenty million people starved to death.

During the 1960s, Mao initiated another drastic domestic program called the **Cultural Revolution**, which was designed to encourage the spontaneous radicalism of the young and the masses against the entrenched party bureaucracy. To revive Mao's popularity, his staunchest supporters, the **Red Guards**, held parades and put up posters criticizing writers, intellectuals, and other enemies of their leader. This led to a wide cult-like following of Mao.

In the early 1970s, Mao reversed a long-standing anti-U.S. policy and opened diplomatic dialogue with the United States. He met with President **Richard Nixon** in 1972, and that began an era of better relations with the capitalist West.

By the mid-1970s, Mao's health began to fail, and he died in September 1976.

NIKITA KHRUSHCHEV won a struggle for control of the Soviet Union after the death of Joseph Stalin. He was the Soviet leader during the grave **Cold War** period.

The son of a coal miner, Khrushchev was born in 1894, in Kalinovka, Ukraine, part of the Russian Empire. He joined the Bolshevik Party in 1918, fought in the Russian Civil War, and rose rapidly within the party.

In 1933, he became second secretary of the Moscow Communist Party and was later elected to full membership of the Party's Central Committee. During the 1930s, Khrushchev was a zealous supporter of Stalin and participated in the purges of the Party's leadership. In 1939, Khrushchev was made a full member of the Politburo—the highest council of the Soviet government.

During World War II, Khrushchev served in the Red Army, and in the postwar era, his political star continued to rise. When Stalin died in March 1953, he was one of five top Soviet officials vying for power. Khrushchev soon emerged in the powerful position of first secretary of the Communist Party.

In 1956, at the Twentieth Party Congress, Khrushchev made a famous speech in which he denounced the crimes of **Stalinism**, the Great Purges, and the "personality cult." The speech provoked an eventual movement to oust Khrushchev from power, but it failed. By the next year, he had removed all his rivals and added the post of premier to his position as head of the party.

For the next several years, Khrushchev pursued contradictory policies, especially in foreign affairs. He widely asserted a doctrine of "peaceful coexistence" with the non-communist world, yet he angered many Western nations with his brutal repression of democracy movements in Eastern Bloc nations such as Hungary. He toured the United States in 1959 and conferred with

President Eisenhower, a move that thawed U.S.-Soviet relations for the first time in more than a decade.

However, in 1961, Khrushchev ordered the construction of a wall separating East and West Berlin, closing off access to freedom in the West by East Germans. The next year, he secretly attempted to base medium-range offensive missiles in **Cuba**, aimed at targets in the United States. After the missiles were detected and President Kennedy demanded they be removed, the two nations stood on the brink of war. Khrushchev finally agreed to remove the missiles if the United States promised to make no further attempt to overthrow Cuba's communist government.

His failures in reforming agriculture policy and the growing rift with communist China led to Khrushchev's downfall. On October 14, 1964, he was removed from power. He died in Moscow in 1971.

Supported by the working classes and buoyed by the popularity of his wife Eva, Argentine dicator **JUAN PERÓN** founded a strongly nationalistic, anti-imperialist movement and engineered great social reforms during his terms as president.

Perón was born into a modest, lower-middle class family in Buenos Aires. He entered military school at age sixteen, and in 1914, he became a lieutenant in an infantry regiment. During the 1930s, he served as a military attaché to Chile, and in the late 1930s and early 1940s, he visited Italy and Germany to observe fascism firsthand.

Perón's rise to power began in 1943 when he was part of a military coup that overthrew the government of **Ramon Castillo**. The next year he was appointed vice president and minister of war. In 1945, he married a young radio and film actress named **Maria Eva Duarte**, who would later achieve great popularity and become known as Evita.

Perón was elected president in 1946 with the support of workers, churchgoers, and recent migrants from the countryside. He quickly used the postwar economic boom to improve the living conditions of workers and laborers at the expense of the large landowners. He also nationalized the foreign-controlled railroads and other utilities as well as financed public works on a large scale.

At the same time, his wife devoted much of her time and energy to social welfare and poverty relief. Extremely popular with the masses, she began to exert a strong influence even within her husband's government. She organized women workers, secured women's right to vote, and allocated large amounts of government funds to social welfare programs.

Perón won reelection in 1951, but the next year, his wife's death due to cancer delivered a severe blow to his government. Over the next few years, the economy deteriorated, and Perón broke with the Catholic Church, losing much support among the military. In 1955, he was overthrown by a military coup and forced into exile.

Perón fled to Paraguay and finally settled in Spain. His **Peróniste** movement remained popular at home, however, and it provided support for him during his time in exile. In his absence, Argentina experienced several years of political, social, and economic upheaval.

In 1971, Perón was allowed to return home, which was quickly seen by his supporters as a chance to save the country from continuing turmoil. He was elected president again in 1973 with 62 percent of the vote. His third wife, **Isabel Martínez de Perón** was elected vice president.

Perón presided over one period of economic recovery, but it was short-lived. He died in 1974 and was succeeded by his wife. She was deposed by the army in 1976.

◆ **GOLDA MEIR** was one of the founders of the state of **Israel** and later served the nation as prime minister.

She was born Golda Mabovitch in 1898 in Kyiv (in present-day Ukraine). When she was eight years old, her family immigrated to Milwaukee, Wisconsin. She was educated at a teacher's seminary and later became a schoolteacher in the same city.

In 1921, she and her husband, Morris Myerson, emigrated to **Palestine** to work and live on a kibbutz. They later changed their surname to a Hebrew one, Meir. During the 1920s, Meir became active in labor relations and in **Zionism**—the movement to create a Jewish state in Palestine. During the 1920s and 1930s, she gained experience as an official of both the Federation of Labor and the Women's Labor Council.

Following World War II, Meir emerged as a forceful spokesperson for the Zionist cause in negotiating with British authorities. She also worked for the release of the many Jewish war refugees who had violated British immigration laws by settling in Palestine.

Golda Meir was one of the twenty-five signatories to Israel's **Proclamation of Independence** issued on May 14, 1948. That same year, she was appointed as her country's first ambassador to the Soviet Union. In 1949, she was also elected to sit in the first Israeli Knesset, or Parliament. Then, during the early 1950s, she served as minister of labor and social insurance for the David Ben-Gurion administration (see no. 73), and in 1956, she became minister of foreign affairs, a post she held for ten years.

After retiring from the Foreign Ministry in 1966, she became secretary-general of the Mapai Party and supported Prime Minister Levi Eshkol in party conflicts. After Israel's victory in the Six-Day War in June 1967 against Egypt, Jordan, and Syria, she helped merge the Mapais with two dissident parties into the Israel **Labor Party**.

Upon Eshkol's death in February 1969, Meir became interim prime minister. After the October 1969 elections, she was elected to a full term. During the next four years, she built a solid international reputation as a tough-minded but empathetic leader.

The major event of her administration was the **Yom Kippur War**, which broke out with massive, coordinated Egyptian and Syrian assaults against Israel on October 6, 1973. Israel's lack of readiness for the war, and the number of Israeli casualties, stunned the nation, and Meir formed a new coalition government with great difficulty. Although she and the Labor Party won the elections later that year, she resigned in 1974 in favor of Yitzhak Rabin.

Meir published her autobiography, *My Life*, in 1975, and died in 1978, after a twelve-year battle with leukemia.

RUHOLLAH KHOMEINI led an Islamic revolution that overthrew the shah of Iran and became his nation's ultimate political and religious leader.

Khomeini was born into a family of Shi'ite scholars in the small town of Khomein in present-day Iran. Later he dropped his family name and adopted the name of his native village. Like his father, he moved from theological studies to a career as a teacher of religion. He wrote many works on Islamic law and ethics,

and as he devoted more of his life to religious studies, he began to be called "**ayatollah**," a religious term of distinction.

Throughout the 1940s and 1950s, Khomeini watched as Iran's leader, or shah, **Muhammad Reza Pahlavi** brought the country closer and closer to the United States and other Western nations, turning it into an increasingly secular state.

Beginning in the early 1960s, Khomeini began to criticize the shah's policies, which he claimed were an adulteration of Islam. For his criticisms, Khomeini was exiled from Iran in 1964. He eventually settled in Iraq, where he continued to mobilize and call for the overthrow of the shah.

From the mid-1970s, Khomeini's influence inside Iran grew dramatically because of mounting public dissatisfaction with the shah's regime. When Khomeini was forced to leave Iraq in 1978, he settled in a Paris suburb. From there his supporters relayed his tape-recorded messages to an increasingly aroused Iranian populace, and massive civil unrest in late 1978 forced the shah to leave the country in January 1979.

Khomeini arrived in Tehrān in triumph in February 1979. Later that year, a referendum on a new constitution created an **Islamic Republic** in Iran, with Khomeini named political and religious leader for life. According to Khomeini's dictates, Iranian women were required to wear the veil, Western music and alcohol were banned, and the punishments prescribed by Islamic law were reinstated.

Khomeini's foreign policy included the complete abandonment of the previous shah's pro-Western orientation—especially toward the United States—which had given the shah refuge. In November 1979, Iranian students took fifty-three American hostages from the U.S. embassy in Tehrān, sparking a crisis that would last for 444 days. Khomeini provoked outrage in the West by not demanding that the students free the hostages.

Over the remaining decade of his life, Khomeini consolidated his rule. Proving himself as ruthless as the shah had been, he had thousands killed while stamping out a rebellion of the secular left. Iran's course of economic development foundered under Khomeini's rule, and his pursuit of victory in the Iran-Iraq War ultimately proved futile. Khomeini was able to retain his charismatic hold over Iran's Shi'ite masses until his death, which sparked an outpouring of grief.

ACHMAD SUKARNO was the founder and leader of the Indonesian nationalist movement and became the first president of an independent Indonesia.

Sukarno was born in Java, in the Dutch East Indies, the son of a poor schoolteacher. At the age of fifteen, Sukarno was sent away to secondary school and to lodgings in the home of Omar Said Tjokroaminoto, a prominent civic and religious figure. Tjokroaminoto financed his further education and married him off at age twenty to his own sixteen-year-old daughter, Siti Oetari.

Endowed with a commanding presence and supreme self-confidence, Sukarno helped form the radical **Indonesian Nationalist Party** in 1927. He was imprisoned for his activities by the Dutch colonial authorities from 1929 to 1931, and after that, he was exiled to Sumatra. He returned to Jakarta in 1942 after the Japanese occupation, which he supported in return for their recognition of his leadership of the nationalist movement. By the end of the war, when the collapse of Japan became imminent, Sukarno declared Indonesia's independence in August 1945.

As president of the shaky new republic, Sukarno united the resistance forces against the Netherlands, who were anxious to reclaim their former colony. After four years, the nationalist movement succeeded, and the Dutch formally transferred sovereignty in December 1949. As Indonesia's first president, Sukarno's task was to unify a disparate population scattered across islands that extended over more than three thousand miles in the Pacific and Indian oceans.

During the first several years of his reign, there were impressive gains in health, education, and cultural self-awareness. However, at the same time, the Indonesian economy foundered while Sukarno conducted numerous receptions, banquets, concerts, and other expensive cultural events.

In the late 1950s, regional and factional problems led Sukarno to replace the 1945 constitution, dissolve parliamentary democracy, and replace it with so-called guided democracy, in which he would become dictator. Sukarno soon increased his country's ties to **communist China**, and his protestations of political "neutralism" were offset by his increasingly virulent anti-Western foreign policy. In 1963, he declared himself president for life. In January 1965, Indonesia formally withdrew from the United Nations because the world organization supported Malaysia, which Sukarno had vowed to "crush."

During the mid-1960s, Sukarno's personal and political excesses—and a corruption scandal in his cabinet—induced a continuous serious state of national crisis. In 1965, he narrowly escaped a coup d'état by a clique of communist conspirators. The coup inspired students to riot in the streets, and anti-military forces led by General **Hadji Suharto** restored order after massacring hundreds of communist sympathizers.

In 1966, Sukarno was forced to delegate wide powers to Suharto, who subsequently became acting president. Sukarno lived under house arrest until his death in 1970.

During **HIROHITO'S** turbulent sixty-three-year reign, Japan went from a military and imperialist power bent on dominating Asia to a defeated, devastated nation that caused the role of the Japanese emperor to change forever.

Michinomiya Hirohito was born in Tokyo, the 124th direct descendant of Jimmu, Japan's first emperor. Hirohito was the eldest son of Crown Prince Yoshihito, and would later become the future Emperor Taishō.

In 1921, Hirohito visited Europe, becoming the first Japanese crown prince to travel abroad. For the first time, the young man experienced personal freedom, visiting museums, fishing in a Scottish lake, and shopping in Paris. When he returned to Japan, he was named prince regent when his father retired due to mental illness. In 1924, Hirohito married the princess **Nagako Kuni**. In 1926, Hirohito's father died, and Hirohito was crowned emperor.

Though the Japanese constitution granted Hirohito supreme authority, in practice he merely ratified the policies of his ministers and advisers. His reign was marked by rapid militarization, and aggressive wars against **Manchuria** in 1931 and **China** in 1937. Then, in 1941, Japan shocked the world with a surprise attack on U.S. military forces in **Pearl Harbor**, Hawaii, provoking a war with America and dragging Japan into World War II.

Some historians assert that Hirohito did not want war with the United States and that he opposed Japan's alliance with Germany and Italy. However, he was powerless against the militarists who dominated the armed forces and the government. Others believe that Hirohito might have been planning Japan's expansionist policies from 1931 until World War II. Wherever the truth lies, Hirohito made an unprecedented radio broadcast announcing Japan's unconditional surrender to the Allies on August 15, 1945, after atomic bombs were dropped on both Hiroshima and Nagasaki. For many Japanese, this was the first time they ever heard their emperor speak.

In a second historic broadcast made on January 1, 1946, Hirohito repudiated the traditional quasi-divine status of Japan's emperors. The constitution of 1946 made him "symbol of the state and of the unity of the people." Hirohito's new role was instrumental in America's occupation, and it was a successful program for the democratization of Japan.

After the war, many long-standing royal traditions were set aside. The emperor became known as a marine biologist, a family figure, and a greeter of foreign heads of state. He allowed photographs of his family to be taken. In 1959, his oldest son, Crown Prince Akihito, married a commoner, Shōda Michiko, breaking a 1,500-year tradition.

In 1971, Hirohito toured Europe, becoming the first reigning Japanese monarch to travel abroad. In 1975, he made a state visit to the United States. Upon his death in 1989, Akihito succeeded him as emperor.

Sweden's **DAG HAMMAR-SKJÖLD** served as the second secretary-general of the **United Nations**, and he greatly enhanced the prestige and effectiveness of the world organization.

Dag Hammarskjöld was the fourth son of Hjalmar Hammarskjöld, prime minister of Sweden during World War I, and he was brought up in the university town of Uppsala. By the age of twenty-five, he had earned a bachelor of arts degree in economics and had received his bache-

lor of law degree. He later taught political economics at Stockholm University before he went on to join the Swedish civil service.

In 1947, he was appointed to the Foreign Office, where he was responsible for all economic questions as undersecretary. He was a delegate to the Paris conference in 1947 when the Marshall Plan machinery was established. In 1951, Hammarskjöld was chosen to be vice chair of Sweden's delegation to the United Nations (UN) General Assembly, of which he became chair in 1952.

On April 10, 1953, five months after the resignation of Norway's Trygve Lie as secretary-general, Hammarskjöld was elected to the office for a five-year term. In September 1957, he was reelected to a second five-year term.

During his tenure as secretary-general, Hammarskjöld carried out many responsibilities for the United Nations to support war prevention programs and to serve the other aims of the UN Charter. For several years, he was most concerned with the **Middle East** tensions between Israel and the Arab nations, and he advocated for peaceful conditions in the area. In 1956, he helped formulate the resolution of the **Suez Canal** crisis between Egypt and Western nations.

In 1955, following his visit to Beijing, China released fifteen detained American fliers who had served under the United Nations Command in the Korean War. As secretary-general, Hammarskjöld traveled to many countries around the world. He had a reputation for combining great moral force with personal subtlety when dealing with international challenges. When the **Belgian Congo** became the independent Republic of the Congo on June 30, 1960, he sent UN forces to mitigate the civil strife that had erupted there. In September 1960, the Soviet Union denounced his action and demanded his removal from office. Hammarskjöld insisted, however, he had the authority to take emergency action without prior approval by the Security Council or the General Assembly. Later, the General Assembly, in an overwhelming vote, approved of Hammarskjöld's actions in the Congo.

Hammarskjöld made four trips to the Congo as part of United Nations operations there. In returning from his fourth trip on September 18, 1961, he was killed in a plane crash. He was posthumously awarded the **Nobel Peace Prize**.

As the first Black African to lead his country to independence from British colonial rule, **KWAME NKRUMAH** inspired a generation of Black African leaders.

Nkrumah was born in the British colony of the Gold Coast (present-day Ghana). Baptized and educated as a Roman Catholic, he later taught at Catholic junior schools and at a seminary until his increasing interest in politics led him to pursue further studies in the United States.

After teaching political science for a time, Nkrumah left the United States in May 1945, and went to England. In London, he met several Black African leaders campaigning for independence from British colonial rule.

Nkrumah returned home in 1947, and he became president of the newly formed **United Gold Coast Convention Party** (UGCC). Nkrumah soon began an intense campaign for self-rule. Boycotts of European goods were initiated, labor strikes became commonplace, and work slowdowns began. When extensive riots occurred in February 1948, the British briefly arrested Nkrumah and other UGCC leaders.

By 1949, Nkrumah had become impatient with what he felt was the slowness of the independence movement. So, in June, he formed the more radical **Convention Peoples' Party** (CPP). In January 1950, he began a campaign of "positive action," involving nonviolent protests, strikes, and noncooperation with the British colonial authorities. Nkrumah was again arrested, and this time he was sentenced to one year in prison.

In 1951, the CPP won an overwhelming victory in the legislative elections, and the British were forced to release Nkrumah from prison. In 1952, the assembly elected him to be the first prime minister of the Gold Coast.

In March 1957, the Gold Coast became the first Black African colony to achieve independence, adopting the name Ghana for the new nation, and Nkrumah became its leader. His style of government proved to be authoritarian. However, his popularity rose as new roads, schools, and health facilities were built, and as the policy of **Africanization** created better lives for the people. In addition, Nkrumah traveled widely, encouraging other African states to become independent.

By the early 1960s, Nkrumah's government had become involved in magnificent but often ruinous development projects, and the once prosperous country became crippled with foreign debt. Contraction of the economy led to widespread labor unrest and to a general strike in September 1961.

In August 1962, Nkrumah survived the first of several assassination attempts. Early in 1964, he declared Ghana officially a one-party state, banned all opposition parties, and named himself president for life. However, by 1966, he had become so unpopular that in February, while he was visiting Beijing, the army and police in Ghana deposed him and seized power. He found asylum in Guinea, and later moved to Romania, where he died of cancer in 1972.

RONALD REAGAN parlayed a career in Hollywood into politics, rising to become president of the United States as the leader of a conservative "revolution" during the 1980s.

Reagan was born in Tampico, Illinois, in 1911. After college, he embarked on a career as a radio sports announcer. In 1937, he was signed to a movie contract and went to Hollywood. Over the next thirty years, he starred in several B-list movies and hosted two dramatic television series. During this period, he was married twice: first to actress Jane Wyman, and then after their divorce, to actress Nancy Davis.

A one-time liberal Democrat, Reagan became a **Republican** and a leading conservative in 1962. In 1966, he was elected governor of California and reelected to a second term in 1970.

After failing twice to gain the Republican presidential nomination, Reagan succeeded in winning in 1980. At sixty-nine years old, Reagan was one of the oldest candidates to run for office. However, his exuberance and optimism during the campaign overcame voter doubts, and his criticisms of an increasingly unpopular president, Jimmy Carter, hit home with many voters. Reagan won the election handily with 489 electoral votes to only 49 for Carter.

Two months after assuming office, Reason was nearly killed when an assassin shot him at close range as he was leaving a Washington hotel. His good humor, courage, and remarkable recovery engendered much good will with the American people.

Reagan came to office promising to cut taxes, trim what he believed to be wasteful government programs, and restore American prestige abroad. By the mid-1980s, he had fulfilled many of his promises. At the same time, Reagan also dramatically increased defense spending, a move that many heavily criticized because they believed it would cause enormous budget deficits. That claim proved to be correct.

However, despite a brief recession in 1982, Reagan remained immensely popular. In 1984, he won reelection by the largest landslide in history, defeating Democrat Walter Mondale by 17 million votes.

During his second term, Reagan surprised many people by developing a strong working partnership with Mikhail Gorbachev, the new leader of the Soviet Union. The two reached agreements on destroying medium-range missiles, dramatically eased East-West tensions, and paved the way for the eventual end of the Cold War.

Reagan's second term was marked by some controversy, especially due to the Iran-Contra Affair, during which Reagan's subordinates took money from illegal arms sales to Iran and used them to fund a counterrevolutionary Nicaraguan group despite Congressional prohibition.

However, when he left office in 1989, Reagan remained hugely popular with the American people. In 1994, many Americans were saddened to learn that he was suffering from Alzheimer's disease. Reagan died in 2004.

No one in twentieth-century American politics had a more spectacular rise or a more dramatic fall than **RICHARD NIXON**, who in 1974 became the first U.S. president to resign from office.

Richard Nixon was born in Yorba Linda, California. He entered politics in his home state in 1946, running as a **Republican** and winning a seat in Congress. In 1950, he won a Senate race against the incumbent Democrat, Helen Gahagan Douglas.

In 1952, Nixon continued his meteoric rise by being picked as Republican presidential nominee Dwight D. Eisenhower's running mate. Eisenhower was elected twice, and during Nixon's eight years as vice president, he did not assume any significant responsibilities.

Nixon received his party's presidential nomination in 1960 and ran against Democrat **John F. Kennedy**, to whom he lost by a very small margin. Eight years later, Nixon made a startling political comeback and captured the Republican presidential nomination. He then defeated Democrat **Hubert Humphrey** in a race that was nearly as close as the one he lost to Kennedy.

Nixon arrived in office at a time when the country was torn apart by the **Vietnam War** and beset with domestic unrest and violence. Aiming to achieve "peace with honor" in Vietnam, Nixon gradually reduced U.S. troop strength there while also escalating the war into neighboring nations such as Cambodia. Eventually, in January 1973,

a peace agreement was signed in Paris that ended U.S. involvement in the war. In terms of domestic affairs, his administration instituted numerous reforms for social welfare, law enforcement, and environmental policy.

In 1972, Nixon was reelected in a landslide over **George McGovern**. In early 1973, however, his second administration began to unravel. On June 17, 1972, five employees of Nixon's reelection committee had been arrested in a break-in for trying to plant surveillance equipment inside the Democratic Party National Headquarters in the **Watergate** building in Washington, DC. Evidence was later uncovered that linked several top White House aides with either initiating the break-in or with later attempts to conceal the fact that the men involved had close ties to the White House.

Nixon insisted that he had no knowledge of the break-in or of a cover-up. However, after investigations by Congress and a special prosecutor, it was revealed that he could be heard on taped conversations in the Oval Office six days after the crime, discussing ways to obstruct the investigation.

In July 1974, the **House Judiciary Committee** voted to impeach Nixon for obstruction of justice. Realizing he would be convicted in the Senate and removed from office, Nixon resigned in disgrace on August 8, 1974.

Nixon returned to California, went into seclusion, and wrote his memoirs. He died in 1994.

◆ Young, vigorous, and charismatic, **JOHN F. KENNEDY** had great promise for his presidency, which would end tragically at the hands of an assassin.

John Fitzgerald Kennedy was born in Brookline, Massachusetts, the son of Joseph Patrick Kennedy, a multimillionaire, and Rose Fitzgerald, daughter of a former Boston mayor.

He graduated from Harvard in 1940 and entered the navy. During World War II, he was cited for heroism for rescuing the crew of his patrol torpedo boat after it had been smashed by a Japanese destroyer. After the war, Kennedy was elected to Congress as a Democrat from Boston. In 1952, he advanced to the Senate, where he served for eight years. In 1953, he married Jacqueline Bouvier, the daughter of a socialite.

In 1960, Kennedy captured the Democratic nomination for president. Millions watched his television debates against Republican candidate **Richard Nixon**. In the closest popular election in history, Kennedy won by the slimmest of margins, and at forty-three, he was the nation's youngest president-elect as well as the first Roman Catholic.

Kennedy came to office promising to bring a new, invigorating spirit to Washington. He initiated programs such as the **Peace Corps** and the **Alliance for Progress** to help bring American democracy to developing nations. He pressed Congress to pass tax cuts and improve labor conditions, and in 1963, he submitted the most sweeping civil rights legislation in the nation's history.

In foreign affairs, Kennedy faced several crises as **Cold War** tensions with the Soviet Union reached new heights. In 1961, he was forced to take responsibility for a botched CIA-backed effort to overthrow Fidel Castro of Cuba. Later that year, the Soviets erected the **Berlin Wall**, cutting off East Berlin from the democratic West. The United States took a strong stand against the Soviet action but was powerless to prevent it.

The most serious crisis of his presidency came in October 1962, when it was discovered that the Soviets were placing medium-range nuclear missiles in **Cuba** ninety miles from America. Kennedy ordered a naval blockade of the island and demanded that Soviet leader **Nikita Khrushchev** (see no. 80) order the missiles to be dismantled. After ten days of tense negotiations, the standoff ended when Khrushchev agreed to the demand in return for a U.S. guarantee to not invade Cuba.

In early planning for the 1964 presidential campaign, Kennedy traveled to Texas in November 1963. While driving in a motorcade through Dallas on November 22, he was shot in the head and died within an hour.

Although many conspiracy theories have been advanced over the years, it is still largely accepted that the crime was committed by a disgruntled ex-Marine-turned-communist named Lee Harvey Oswald, who was also killed two days after supposedly killing Kennedy.

The first woman prime minister of India, **INDIRA GANDHI** dedicated her life to political and social progress in her country.

Indira Gandhi was born in Allahabad, India, the only child of Jawaharlal Nehru, the first prime minister of independent India. She was educated in India and Europe, and then she entered politics. She joined the National Congress Party in 1938 and became active in India's independence movement. In 1942, she married **Feroze Gandhi**, with whom she had two sons.

After India gained independence in 1947, she began to work at her father's side and rose through the ranks of the party. In 1964, upon her father's death, she became minister of information and broadcasting in the government of Prime Minister Lal Bahadur Shastri. When Shastri died in 1966, she became prime minister.

Gandhi gained enormous popularity for her actions during the Pakistani civil war of 1971. With her support, East Pakistanis finally achieved independence and became the nation of Bangladesh. She also earned support by promising to use scientific methods to eradicate poverty.

Gandhi was reelected by a landslide in 1971, but problems began to plague her government. Shortly after the election, her opponent charged that she had violated the election laws, and her leadership became vulnerable. A sharp economic downturn caused by severe droughts led to widespread unrest as well. In June 1975, she declared a national state of emergency in response to what she said was a threat to national security. As a result, political opponents were imprisoned, the press was censored, and civil liberties were limited.

During this period, she also implemented several unpopular policies, including large-scale, voluntary sterilization to control the rising population. When national elections were held in 1977, Gandhi and her party were soundly defeated, and she left office. Later that year, she was briefly jailed on charges of political corruption, and later she was expelled from Parliament.

However, the new government failed to solve India's problems. By 1980, Gandhi had reorganized her party, and in the elections that year, she became prime minister again. When her son **Sanjay**, her chief political adviser, died in a plane crash, she began grooming her older son, **Rajiv**, to be her successor.

Religious disturbances and terrorism caused by separatists beset Gandhi's second term. Several states sought a larger measure of independence from the central government, and **Sikh** extremists in the **Punjab state** violently asserted their demands for an autonomous state. In 1984, she moved vigorously to suppress Sikh insurgents by sending troops to storm the **Golden Temple** in Amritsar, killing more than three hundred people. In retaliation, on October 31, 1984, Sikh members of her security guard shot her to death.

GAMAL ABDEL NASSER rose from a modest upbringing to become president of Egypt, and his efforts to unify the Arab nations made him a national hero and the acknowledged leader of the Arab nations.

Nasser was born in a mud-brick house in Alexandria, Egypt, and his father was in charge of the local post office. From Alexandria, Nasser's father was transferred to Al-Khaṭāṭibah, a squalid delta village, where the young boy began school. He then went to live in Cairo with an uncle and entered the **Cairo Military Academy**, graduating as a second lieutenant. He fought in the unsuccessful Arab war against Israel in 1948.

With three fellow officers, Nasser formed a secret revolutionary organization called the Free Officers, whose aim was to overthrow King Farouk I. After Egypt's humiliation in the war against Israel, the movement grew quickly. In July 1952, Nasser and eighty-nine other **Free Officers** staged an almost bloodless coup d'état that ended with the king and his supporters going into exile. The Revolutionary Command Council took over the country, and General Muḥammad Neguib became president and Nasser became minister of the interior as well as Neguib's deputy. Nasser then engaged in a bitter power struggle with Neguib and replaced him as president in 1954.

In January 1956, Nasser announced a constitution under which Egypt became a socialist Arab state with a one-party political system. Islam became the official state religion. Nasser then began to reduce government corruption and carry out land and social reforms. His announcement in 1956 of his intention to nationalize the Suez Canal was highly popular at home but set off an international crisis. Great Britain, aided by France and Israel, attacked Egypt. But in the aftermath of the brief war, Nasser emerged with undiminished prestige throughout the Arab nations.

With the United States and other Western nations following a strong pro-Israeli policy, Nasser turned toward the Soviet Union for assistance. He purchased arms from the Soviets and used Soviet funds to help construct the Aswān High Dam, which would help introduce modern twentieth-century life to many Egyptian villages.

In 1967, Nasser led the Arab nations against Israel in what became known as the Six-Day War. In the wake of Israel's overwhelming success, Nasser briefly resigned as president, but his continued popularity with the Egyptian people brought him back to power.

Despite his international setbacks, Nasser accomplished much at home during his tenure. He redistributed land, encouraged industrialization, expanded public works, and provided more equitable educational opportunities.

Nasser died of a heart attack in 1970, just one year before the completion of his greatest domestic project, the Aswān High Dam.

As president of Egypt, **ANWAR SADAT** helped end thirty years of Egyptian-Israeli hostilities and brought a measure of peace to the Middle East for the first time in modern history.

Sadat was born in a small village in the Nile delta, the son of a hospital clerk. He graduated from the **Cairo Military Academy** in 1938 and was sent to a distant outpost where he met **Gamal Abdel Nasser** (see no. 92). During World War II, Sadat was imprisoned for plotting to expel the British from Egypt. He escaped, and after the war, he joined Nasser's group, the **Free Officers**, which was dedicated to overthrowing the British-dominated monarchy.

In 1952, Sadat joined the Free Officers' armed coup that resulted in the overthrow of King Farouk. Sadat supported Nasser's election to the presidency in 1956, and over the next decade, served in several important posts, including minister of state. In 1969, Sadat was chosen as Nasser's vice president, and he became president the year after Nasser's death.

In an effort to remove himself from Nasser's huge shadow, Sadat began to decentralize the country's political structure and diversify the economy. He also distanced himself from Nasser's foreign policy by expelling Soviet technicians and advisers from the country and initiating closer ties with the United States.

In 1973, Sadat launched the **Yom Kippur War** against Israel, which caught the Israelis off guard and restored some Egyptian honor that had been lost during the humiliation of the 1967 Six-Day War. With his prestige quite high at home, Sadat made a dramatic turnaround and began to work toward peace in the Middle East. He made a historic visit to Israel in November 1977 and addressed the Israeli Parliament. The trip initiated a series of diplomatic efforts that Sadat continued despite fervent opposition from most of the Arab nations.

U.S. President Jimmy Carter mediated negotiations between Sadat and Israeli Prime Minister **Menachem Begin**, which culminated in the Camp David Accords of September 1978. The agreement established a framework for continuing negotiations that resulted in a peace treaty between Egypt and Israel in March 1979—the first treaty between Israel and any Arab nation. For their efforts, Sadat and Begin shared the **Nobel Peace Prize** in 1978.

At home, Sadat's new relationship with the West and his peace treaty generated domestic opposition, especially among fundamentalist Muslim groups. In 1980 and 1981, Sadat took desperate measures to respond to these internal problems. He negotiated many loans to improve everyday life, while at the same time cracking down on the opposition by outlawing protests. Despite these actions, Sadat was assassinated by Muslim extremists during a military parade in October 1981.

NELSON MANDELA endured lengthy imprisonment during his lifetime struggle against South Africa's **apartheid** system and triumphed by becoming his nation's first elected Black president.

Nelson Rolihlahla Mandela was born in 1918 in Cape of Good Hope, South Africa. He was the son of Chief Henry Mandela of the Tembu people. When he was a young man, Mandela moved to Johannesburg, earned a law degree, and became active in Youth League, a wing of the **African National Congress** (ANC), a Black Nationalist group. In 1949, Mandela became a leader in the ANC and engaged in militant resistance against the new white-ruling National Party's policies of apartheid, which had officially segregated the population and denied Black South Africans the basic rights that white South Africans enjoyed.

In 1953, Mandela was banned for his ANC activities, and in 1956, he was tried for treason. The trial lasted five years, and Mandela was eventually acquitted. During this period, he divorced his first wife and married **Winnie Madikizela-Mandela**, a social worker.

After the **Sharpeville Massacre** in 1960, during which government troops killed and wounded scores of peaceful Black demonstrators, Mandela organized a paramilitary group to engage in guerrilla warfare against the government. In 1962, he was jailed and sentenced to five years in prison. Then in 1963, Mandela and several other men were tried for treason and sabotage. In June 1964, he was convicted and sentenced to life in prison.

Throughout the 1970s and 1980s, Mandela maintained wide support among South Africa's Black population. He also gained further support from the international community, largely due to the efforts of his wife Winnie, who was instrumental in making him the leading symbol of South African repression. By the late 1980s, there was growing international pressure for his release. In 1989, President **F. W. de Klerk** began the process of dismantling apartheid.

Mandela was released from prison in February 1990, as an expression of de Klerk's commitment to change.

Mandela and the ANC began negotiations with the government to end white majority rule in South Africa. Mandela and de Klerk were jointly awarded the **Nobel Peace Prize** in 1993 for their work in bringing about a peaceful transition to non-racial democracy in South Africa.

In South Africa's first multiracial elections in 1994, Mandela was elected president. He investigated human rights violations under apartheid and introduced housing, education, and economic development initiatives designed to improve the living standards of the country's Black population.

In 1996, Mandela and Winnie divorced after she had become a controversial figure, accused of being an accessory to criminal activities committed by her bodyguards. In 1999, Mandela did not seek a second term as president and retired from politics. In his retirement, Mandela advocated for social justice and reconciliation. He died in 2013.

As Great Britain's first woman prime minister, **MARGARET THATCHER'S** rigid approach to policy making and steely self-confidence earned her the title the "Iron Lady" from friend and foe alike.

She was born Margaret Hilda Roberts in Lincolnshire, England. She was educated at Oxford University, where she became interested in politics. In 1951, she married **Denis Thatcher**, a wealthy businessperson.

With her husband's encouragement, Thatcher pursued her political ambitions. In 1959, she became a member of Parliament as a **Conservative**. From 1970 to 1974, she served as minister of education and science under Prime Minister Edward Heath.

In 1975, Thatcher became leader of the Conservative Party—the first woman to hold that position. By the late 1970s, Britain was going through very tough times. In March 1979, Thatcher called for a no-confidence vote in the ruling Labor Party leadership. When elections were held in May, the Conservatives won the majority, and Margaret Thatcher became Great Britain's first woman prime minister.

To boost the economy, she announced lower income tax rates and cut social programs. While this action pleased conservatives, she was also heavily criticized by others for being cold-hearted toward the jobless and the poor.

Unemployment, which had been rising mildly in the late 1970s, climbed dramatically by 1981, spurring riots nationwide. But Thatcher's reaction was to crack down with more police enforcement. During her time in office, she also privatized some nationalized industries and social programs, including education, housing, and healthcare. While Thatcher's policies continued to draw criticism, the economy improved throughout much of the 1980s, and she was given credit for it.

In 1982, Argentine forces occupied the **Falkland Islands**, which were claimed by both Argentina and Great Britain.

Thatcher's government sent a task force to the islands that defeated the Argentineans in a brief war. Her Falkland Islands success, and the economic upturn, allowed Thatcher to lead the Conservatives to a sweeping victory in the elections of 1983, giving her a second term as prime minister.

Throughout the 1980s, Thatcher developed a close working relationship with U.S. President **Ronald Reagan** (see no. 88), who shared many of her conservative views.

Thatcher was also one of the first Western leaders to meet with Soviet president **Mikhail Gorbachev**, after which she announced that he was a leader the West could "do business with."

In 1987, Thatcher won an unprecedented third term as prime minister. However, by 1990, a recession had set in. Controversy over Thatcher's tax policy, and her reluctance to commit Great Britain to full economic integration with Europe, inspired a strong internal challenge to her leadership. She resigned as head of the Conservative Party late in 1990. She was succeeded as leader and prime minister by her protégé, John Major. In 1992, Thatcher was appointed a life peerage, entitling her to sit in the House of Lords. She died of a stroke in 2013.

A lawyer turned revolutionary, **FIDEL CASTRO** transformed Cuba into the first communist nation in the Western Hemisphere.

Fidel Castro was born in the Mayarí municipality, the son of a sugarcane farmer. In his youth, Castro attended Catholic schools and studied law at the University of Havana, graduating in 1950.

After law school, Castro went to work in Havana to help the poor. By the early 1950s, he had come to detest the regime of Cuba's dictator, **Fulgencio Batista**, whose harsh rule favored the wealthy class. Castro became involved in revolutionary politics, and in 1953, he helped lead an unsuccessful attempt to overthrow Batista. Castro was jailed for two years and was released in 1955. He then went into exile to organize a guerrilla campaign to oust the dictator.

In December 1956, a group led by Castro, his brother Raul, and another committed revolutionary, **Ernesto "Che" Guevara**, organized another attempt to overthrow Batista. Once again, they failed, and they retreated to the mountains. For the next two years, with Castro's charismatic leadership, the movement to overthrow the dictatorship gathered support, until finally, on January 1, 1959, they toppled Batista. He fled the country, and Castro and his forces triumphantly entered Havana to take control.

Widely hailed as a liberator, Castro proved to be a tough and often ruthless leader. He collectivized agriculture and took over foreign-owned industries. He instituted sweeping reforms in favor of the poor, disenfranchising the propertied classes, many members of which were fleeing the country. These policies, along with Castro's trade agreement with the **Soviet Union** in February 1960, deepened distrust in the United States, which broke diplomatic relations with Cuba in 1961.

In April 1961, the United States organized an invasion of Cuban exiles at the **Bay of Pigs**, which was a disastrous failure. A year later, the world came to the brink of nuclear war when the Soviet Union—the island nation's chief supporter and trade partner—placed nuclear weapons there that could reach the United States. The crisis was defused following negotiations between the superpowers and the removal of the missiles.

Castro maintained his iron grip over the next three decades. While the quality of life for the poorest people improved, there was no denying that Cubans had lost many of their basic freedoms as Castro refused to allow any democratic opposition to his rule.

When the Soviet Union collapsed in 1991, Cuba entered a crisis period. Popular unrest grew in the face of extreme austerity measures. In desperate need of foreign capital, Castro opened Cuba to foreign investment and promoted tourism while further clamping down on dissent. Though his prestige dwindled dramatically, Castro remained a symbol of revolutionary progress for many of Cuba's poorest citizens.

Castro remained president until his health began to deteriorate, and then his brother Raul took over as president. Fidel Castro died in 2016.

MIKHAIL GORBACHEV brought dramatic changes to the Soviet Union during the 1980s, and then allowed a wildfire democracy movement to sweep across Eastern Europe and end the Cold War.

Born to farming parents in a Russian village along the Volga River, Mikhail Gorbachev also worked in the fields as a young boy. His father was a Communist Party official, and by 1946, the young man had joined the Komsomol, or Communist Youth League. Gorbachev went on to study law at Moscow State University and graduated in 1955. During the early 1950s, he also joined the Communist Party and married Raisa Maksimovna Titorenko.

Returning to Stavropol, he began to move up within the Party ranks, and by 1978, he had moved to Moscow to further his career. In 1980, Gorbachev became a full member of the **Politburo**, the national Soviet governing body, and by 1983, he had been given full guardianship over the economy, which had been stagnating for many years. In 1985, despite his relatively young age, Gorbachev succeeded Konstantin Chernenko as general secretary of the Communist Party—the nation's top leadership position.

From the beginning, Gorbachev cultivated warmer relations and more open trade between the developed Eastern and Western nations. He also helped usher in a new era of good relations with the United States by holding a series of summit talks with President **Ronald Reagan** that led both countries to sign an Intermediate Nuclear Forces (INF) arms limitation treaty in 1987. Most dramatically, in 1989, when democracy movements swept across Eastern Europe in Soviet-dominated countries, Gorbachev refused to follow the actions of previous leaders and suppress them. By not taking action, he effectively helped end the Cold War, and the Berlin Wall fell that year.

Internally, Gorbachev embarked on a dual policy of social and political reform: glasnost, or openness, and perestroika, or economic restructuring. Though the changes greatly democratized Soviet politics and increased cultural and social freedoms, they produced few economic benefits. At the same time, the reforms unleashed long-suppressed ethnic conflicts and separatist movements.

The signing of a treaty that transferred much power to the republics within the Soviet Union led hard-liners in Gorbachev's government to temporarily oust him. In the aftermath, Gorbachev aligned himself with **Boris Yeltsin**, who had helped thwart the takeover. Gorbachev resigned from the Communist Party, and though he agreed to even greater power sharing with the republics, these efforts failed to prevent the Soviet Union's disintegration. On December 25, 1991, Gorbachev resigned, and a week later, the Soviet Union ceased to exist.

Mikhail Gorbachev was awarded the **Nobel Peace Prize** in 1990 for his striking achievements in helping to end the forty-year-long Cold War.

Iraqi dictator **SADDAM HUSSEIN'S** invasion of Kuwait in 1990 led to the formation of the first post-Cold War UN military force and resulted in the **Gulf War**.

Hussein was born into a Muslim peasant family in northern Iraq in 1937. He joined the **Ba'ath Socialist Party** in 1957 and participated in several attempts to kill Iraqi prime minister Abdul Kassem. Hussein was imprisoned, but he escaped to Syria and then Egypt when Kassem was overthrown in a coup. Hussein returned to Iraq in 1963, when the Ba'athists briefly grabbed power.

By 1968, Hussein had risen to a top position within the Ba'athists, and that year, they seized control of Iraq. In 1969, Hussein became deputy chair of the **Revolutionary Command Council**, the country's new ruling body in the government of Aḥmad Ḥasan al-Bakr.

Hussein became president in 1979 when al-Bakr retired. Hussein quickly focused on strengthening the Iraqi oil industry and gaining a greater foothold in the Arab nations. Internally, he used secret police to suppress any opposition to his rule; he also engaged in a brutal repression of the rebellious **Kurdish** minority, wiping out thousands of Kurds in villages in northern Iraq.

In 1980, Hussein began a bitter war against neighboring Iran to gain control of the Strait of Hormuz. The **Iran-Iraq War** lasted eight years and was fought to a stalemate. Finally, in 1988, it ended with a cease-fire agreement.

Then on August 2, 1990, Hussein sanctioned an Iraqi invasion of neighboring Kuwait. He planned to use that country's oil revenues to bolster Iraq's economy, but the invasion brought about UN sanctions. Hussein ignored appeals to withdraw his forces, despite the buildup of a large U.S.-led multinational military force in Saudi Arabia.

When Hussein refused to relent, the UN forces intervened on January 16, 1991. In a six-week-long war, the multinational coalition drove Iraq's armies out of Kuwait. Hussein's troops surrendered in February 1991.

Hussein was immediately confronted with civil war as his army retreated. Shi'ite Muslims and Kurds rebelled, but Hussein put down their uprisings, causing thousands to flee to refugee camps along the country's northern border.

In the aftermath of the Gulf War, a special UN delegation was sent to oversee the destruction and removal of all Iraqi nonconventional weapons. Iraq was also prohibited from producing chemical and nuclear weapons. Numerous sanctions were leveled on the country pending compliance, causing severe shortages of food and medicine and further weakening the economy. Initially Iraq refused to disclose all its nuclear sites, but when the allies threatened to resume an air offensive, the Iraqis supplied the necessary information.

In 1995, Hussein held a national referendum and was confirmed as president for seven more years. In April 2003, U.S. and British forces invaded Iraq, and Hussein went into hiding. He was captured in December that year. In 2006, he was convicted of crimes against humanity and executed.

A shipyard worker and founder of Poland's first independent trade union, **LECH WAŁĘSA** played a major role in ending communism and bringing about the rise of democracy in his country.

Wałęsa was one of eight children born into a worker-peasant family in Popowo, Poland. In 1967, he became an electrician in the **Lenin Shipyards** in Gdańsk, and in 1970, he participated in the large-scale shipyard demonstrations against the government's decision to increase food prices.

In 1976, Wałęsa emerged as an anti-government union activist, and as a result, he was fired from his job. In 1980, when worker strikes once again occurred, Wałęsa scaled the fence at the Lenin Shipyards to join the workers occupying the site. He took charge of the strike and negotiated an agreement with the government that would grant workers the right to organize freely and to strike. The shipyard strike influenced workers and farmers throughout Poland.

Wałęsa then founded the independent trade union Solidarność, or Solidarity. In a short time, some ten million Polish workers from around the country had registered as members. Wałęsa's charismatic leadership of Solidarity brought him immediate national and international recognition.

By 1981, worker dissatisfaction and social unrest were increasing, and the Soviet Union was putting pressure on the Polish government to crack down. Defense Minister **Wojciech Jaruzelski** was appointed prime minister, and in December, he imposed martial law and outlawed Solidarity. Wałęsa was arrested and detained for seven months. For the next six years, he was either under arrest or watched closely by the secret police. In 1983, he was awarded the **Nobel Peace Prize**, which only angered the Polish government even further.

By December 1988, it was clear that the social unrest and poor economic conditions could not continue. The ruling Communist Party invited Wałęsa to join negotiations, which lasted for fifty-nine days. In the end, Solidarity was legalized, and the government sanctioned free elections for a limited number of seats in the upper house of the Sejm, or Parliament. In June 1989, Solidarity won an overwhelming majority of those seats, and after Wałęsa refused to form a coalition government with the Communists, Parliament was forced to accept a Solidarity-led government.

In 1990, Wałęsa ran successfully for president. He then led the country through industrial privatization, and Poland's first set of totally free elections. He also began international relations with the newly emerging states of Central and Eastern Europe as well as with the Western powers.

Wałęsa's confrontational style, and his refusal to approve a relaxation of Poland's prohibitions on abortion, eroded his popularity late in his term. In 1995, he sought reelection, but was narrowly defeated by the former communist, **Aleksander Kwaśniewski.**

As the first woman chancellor of Germany, **ANGELA MERKEL** guided the European Union (EU) through challenges for nearly sixteen years and established herself as the most powerful woman in the world.

Born Angela Dorothea Kasner in 1954 in Hamburg, West Germany, Merkel was the eldest of three children. When she was only a few months old, the family moved to a rural area north of Berlin in East Germany. Merkel excelled in school, winning prizes in Russian and mathematics, and after finishing secondary school, she studied physics at Karl Marx University (present-day University of Leipzig). After earning her first degree in 1978, she worked as a chemist at the Central Institute for Physical Chemistry until 1990, and during that time, she earned her doctorate in quantum chemistry in 1986.

The fall of the Berlin Wall in 1989 inspired Merkel to get involved in politics. She joined Democratic Awakening, a new political party, and was appointed press spokesperson for the party in February 1990 before it merged with the larger national party, the Christian Democratic Union (CDU). That same year, in the first federal election following the reunification of Germany, Merkel was elected to Germany's parliament, called the Bundestag. She was appointed as minister for women and youth in 1991 and in 1994 was appointed minister for the environment, nature conservation and nuclear safety. In 1998, she became the first woman leader of the CDU, and after the 2005 federal election, she was appointed chancellor of Germany. In addition to being the first woman chancellor, she was also the youngest and the first person who had been raised in East Germany to hold the office.

The early years of Merkel's chancellorship were marred by rising unemployment worldwide and growing economic instability. After the financial crash of 2008, several countries in the EU—including Greece, Portugal, Ireland, Spain, and Cyprus—found themselves in a debt crisis when they were unable to repay their government debt, which in turn, threatened to devalue the euro, the currency shared by most EU member states. Merkel negotiated a major stimulus plan to allay the threat to the euro and backed loans to struggling EU countries while taking tough austerity measures on the indebted countries. Leading the EU through the crisis with a level head, many now credit Merkel with saving the European currency.

Merkel navigated another major crisis in 2015, when millions of migrants and refugees from Syria, Afghanistan, Nigeria, Pakistan, and other Middle Eastern and African countries flooded into Europe seeking asylum after fleeing war and persecution in their home countries. While many countries in Central Europe refused to take in refugees, Merkel and the German government decided to suspend its enforcement of EU asylum rules and accept all refugees. Merkel called on Germans to contribute to a *Wilkommenskultur*, or welcoming culture, and many Germans offered refugees accommodations, supplies, and monetary support. However, some Germans rejected this, and the crisis sparked a rise in nationalism and xenophobia in the country. Merkel stood by her decision and was praised all over the world as a steady and fair leader, who demonstrates humanity while facing a tough situation.

Merkel served four terms as chancellor. She stepped down at the end of 2021.

TRIVIA QUESTIONS

TEST YOUR knowledge and challenge your friends with the following questions. The answers are contained in the biographies noted.

1. Which Babylonian ruler devised a "code" that governed all aspects of life for his people? (See no. 3)

2. Which ancient Greek political leader led Athens during the height of that city-state's imperial power and cultural greatness? (See no. 8)

3. Who was the ruthless fifth-century warrior who led his forces in a series of campaigns that nearly destroyed Western Christendom? (See no. 15)

4. How did a Danish king unite the Danish and English people and become the first person since the fall of Rome to rule all of England? (See no. 23)

5. Which outstanding French ruler consolidated the power of the monarchy and turned his kingdom into a fully organized state? (See no. 29)

6. How did the first woman medieval ruler bring together three Scandinavian countries to form a union that would last for more than one hundred and thirty years? (See no. 32)

7. Why did a famous Aztec emperor welcome a Spanish conqueror and his army only to allow them to capture his capital city and eventually destroy his empire? (See no. 35)

8. Where did an eighteenth-century Russian tsar build his new capital to give his country a desired "window to the West"? (See no. 42)

9. Which general transformed the French Revolutionary Republic into an empire and, in the process, conquered much of Europe? (See no. 48)

10. When did a great Italian patriot lead his armed forces to a victory that unified Italy for the first time since the days of the Roman Empire? (See no. 53)

11. Which U.S. president was unable to convince the senate to approve a treaty and allow the United States to enter the world's first international organization? (See no. 60)

12. What twentieth-century European agreement became a symbol of appeasement and failed to prevent the outbreak of another world war? (See no. 65)

13. Who served his nation as its leader longer than any other person and led his country through one of its most turbulent periods in history? (See no. 71)

14. What crisis nearly brought two superpowers to the brink of war? (See no. 80)

15. Why was a U.S. president forced to become the first chief executive to resign? (See no. 89)

16. Where did a lawyer-turned-revolutionary establish the first communist nation in the Western Hemisphere? (See no. 96)

PROJECT SUGGESTIONS

1. Choose one of the world leaders from this book and write a one-page fictional diary entry for one day in that person's life. Pick a day that had some significance for the individual. For example, the day they won an important military battle, or the day they were awarded a Nobel Prize. Or, choose a day on which the person faced a severe defeat or was frustrated in some way by their lack of success. Describe the person's thoughts and feelings in as much detail as you can.

2. Arrange a "meeting" between two leaders in this book who could never have met in real life. Choose them from different eras and perhaps even different walks of life (for example, Lorenzo the Magnificent and Napoleon I, or Peter the Great and Saint John XXIII). Imagine what their meeting would be like. Write one to two pages describing the scenario of their meeting and create a dialogue between the two leaders. What kinds of questions do you think they would ask each other? Would they approve of the things that the other had done? Be as imaginative as you can.

INDEX

OUT NOW:

100 African Americans Who Shaped American History
100 American Women Who Shaped American History
100 Americans Who Shaped American History
100 Athletes That Shaped Sports History
100 Artists Who Shaped World History
100 Authors Who Shaped World History
100 Baseball Legends Who Shaped Sports History
100 Battles That Shaped World History
100 Books That Shaped World History
100 Colonial Leaders Who Shaped World History
100 Disasters That Shaped World History
100 Events That Shaped World History
100 Explorers Who Shaped World History
100 Families Who Shaped World History
100 Folk Heroes Who Shaped World History
100 Great Cities of World History
100 Hispanic and Latino Americans Who Shaped American History
100 Immigrants Who Shaped American History
100 Inventions That Shaped World History
100 Medical Milestones That Shaped World History
100 Men Who Shaped World History
100 Military Leaders Who Shaped World History
100 Native Americans Who Shaped American History
100 Natural Wonders of the World
100 Relationships That Shaped World History
100 Scientists Who Shaped World History
100 Ships and Planes That Shaped World History
100 Spiritual Leaders Who Shaped World History
100 Wars That Shaped World History
100 Women Who Shaped World History